D1070031

FRAUD 101

IDENTITY THEFT, FRAUD, AND INTERNET SCAMS & SCHEMES

FRAUD 101

Identity Theft, Fraud, and Internet Scams & Schemes

∎ ∎ ∎

Staff Sergeant
Terry Keighley
RCMP Veteran Member

GENERAL STORE PUBLISHING HOUSE
499 O'Brien Road, Box 415
Renfrew, Ontario, Canada K7V 4A6
Telephone (613) 432-7697 or 1-800-465-6072
www.gsph.com

ISBN 978-1-897113-71-4

Cover illustration, design and layout: Magdalene Carson / New Leaf Publication
Design
Printed by Custom Printers of Renfrew Ltd., Renfrew, Ontario
Printed and bound in Canada

Library and Archives Canada Cataloguing in Publication
Keighley, Terry, 1942-
     Fraud 101 : identity theft, fraud and Internet scams and schemes / Terry
Keighley.

ISBN 978-1-897113-71-4

     1. Identity theft--Canada. 2. Fraud--Canada. 3. Swindlers and
swindling--Canada. I. Title.
HV6699.C3K45 2009   364.16'30971   C2007-907056-6

This book is dedicated to daughters Taija and Katriina,
with special thanks for their typing and grammatical skills,
and to my son, Christian, with a pat on the back
for keeping us laughing at all times.
And to all those who encouraged and helped me
—it was greatly appreciated.

TABLE OF CONTENTS

FOREWORD

I have known Staff Sergeant Terry Keighley for more than twenty-five years. During the decade of the 1980s, I was privileged to have partnered with him in solving several complicated white-collar crimes. His book accurately reflects many of the fraudulent schemes, both personal and commercial, that are prevalent today.

Here we are, just eight years into the twenty-first century, and *fraud* has already engrained itself as **the** *crime of the new millennium*. Millions of personal and corporate dollars are lost each year to enterprising first-time offenders and well-organized criminal gangs. Canada's financial system is under serious attack by sophisticated fraudsters who use high technology to "skim" credit and debit card data from ATMs and point-of-sale terminals. The same high-tech criminals also "phish" for and obtain confidential data using computers and the Internet. They steal identities to commit fraud. They divert mail and intercept cheques in order to alter them for their own financial benefit.

Fraud is pervasive. The types of fraud committed today are near endless. Although considered a crime against interests in property, rather than a crime against persons, fraud can be as harmful and ruinous as a physical attack. Nervous breakdowns, breakup of families, failed businesses, forfeiture of real estate, or loss of lifetime savings are often the result of well-orchestrated schemes to defraud.

Knowledge is the consumer's best tool to combat fraud. Terry's book contains enough information to put individuals, governments, and the corporate sector on high alert and to help them learn *how **not** to be a victim of fraud.*

Sergeant Ron Bélanger, Fraud Consultant
Veteran, Royal Canadian Mountain Police (Commercial Crime Section)
Former Chair, Canadian Bankers Association Security Sub-Committee
Former Executive, International Association of Financial Crime Investigators (Central Canada)
Recognized internationally "For Excellence of Performance in Administration of Justice."

Sharing

This book is about sharing the knowledge that I have gained through serving Canada as a member of the Royal Canadian Mounted Police. It is also about sharing the experience I have acquired investigating financial and white-collar crimes over the past two decades. We all know somebody who has been victimized by fraudsters, and we have all been approached by individuals offering a heck of a lot of something for a lot of nothing, or almost nothing. For reasons I have never really understood, some of us take the bait, and some of us never get hooked.

These frauds, scams, and schemes appear to attack and land individuals from all areas of the social and economic spectrum; wealth and education are not always a defence against fraud. If you have wealth and assets, you may also become a high-end target; make sure that when the bad guys set the traps, you are not the one who gets caught.

Look at it this way: fraud perpetrated against individuals can run from very simplistic to quite sophisticated. At the same time, the criminals involved in fraud can run from very simple to somewhat sophisticated in their thinking. Now, oddly enough, the low-level, unsophisticated fraudster usually hits more frequently, and just keeps on going. Some of these guys have five or ten priors for fraudulent-type crimes. Nothing stops them—it's the old try, try, again approach, which, with your help, eventually makes these guys rich. Who needs the lottery? They have you.

The other side of the coin is this: If you will stop assisting the bad guys when they attempt to take your property or money, then I will give you the information you need to stop them dead in their tracks, or at least force them off you and on to their next target (hopefully not your unaware neighbour).

THE TOP TEN LIST

(FROM THE HOME OFFICE IN BRANTFORD)

The TOP TEN Reasons Why You Will Never Get Stung by Identity Theft or Fraud

#10 You do not have a bank account.

#9 You do not have a credit card in your name.

#8 You live in your mother's basement.

#7 You have no computer . . . no Internet . . . no life.

#6 You are forty and single.

#5 You use only cash.

#4 You do not have a driver's licence or a car.

#3 You bought my book.

#2 You actually read it.

And the number one reason why Identity Theft or Fraud will never grab you by the wallet is . . .

#1 You carry stolen identification!

Staff Sergeant Terry Keighley
RCMP Veteran Member

THE HEADLINES

No matter where you live in North America, it's difficult to read the newspaper or listen to the news and not encounter stories about fraud and identity theft. In fact, without fraud or identity theft, there would hardly be any news. Let me give you a few examples:

NINETEEN-YEAR-OLD UNIVERSITY STUDENT RECEIVES NOTIFICATION FROM A BANK THANKING HER FOR UTILIZING HER PRE-APPROVED MORTGAGE

RCMP INDICATES THAT FOR 2007 IDENTITY THEFT LOSSES IN CANADA ARE NOW MEASURED IN THE BILLIONS

WIDOW DISCOVERS HER TOWN HOUSE HAS BEEN SOLD WITHOUT HER KNOWLEDGE

POLICE INDICATE THAT IDENTITY THEFT HAS BECOME THE CRIME WAVE OF THE NEW MILLENNIUM

THIRTY-FIVE INDIVIDUALS HAVE THEIR CREDIT CARDS SKIMMED AT LOCAL GAS STATION

EIGHTY-YEAR-OLD COUPLE RECEIVES STATEMENT FROM BANK INDICATING THEY HAVE A $350,000 MORTGAGE ON THEIR HOME

DUMPSTER DIVERS REMOVE PERSONAL MAIL FROM APARTMENT BUILDING GARBAGE

CANADIAN BANKS INDICATE THAT DEBIT CARD SKIMMING IS EVER-INCREASING

Now, you could take the position that none of this stuff will ever happen to you, and you may be right. But come on, do you really think that the people who have already been bruised and battered by fraud, and had some or all of their hard-earned cash disappear, thought it would happen to them? The short answer is no, of course not. Do they wish that they had an understanding of who, what, why, and how? You can bet your ass-sets they do. But some of us are always a step behind; I have no idea why. I do know that you must get up to speed on this fraud stuff, or you might eventually be spending a lot of your time being part of tomorrow's headlines!

Canada's Criminal Code describes "fraud" as deceit, falsehood, or other fraudulent means. It would be pretty hard to go through life and not come up against one of these three aspects of fraud. Have you never bumped up against one of the three at work, at school, at home, in a relationship . . . okay, I won't go there . . . but you must admit, the potential for fraud is everywhere. Now, when somebody utilizes these tricks to try and take your money, property, or valuables, and they perpetrate this fraud using another aspect of today's criminal tool kit, identity fraud, this can become overwhelming. In today's world, you have to know what the bad guys are doing and how they are doing it. This is a very slippery slope. You have to get up to speed, or you are going to go over the edge.

INTRODUCTION

I have written this book in an attempt to educate you, the public at large, about the serious consequences of being victimized by criminals perpetrating a large number of fraudulent schemes. Although some of these schemes are separate from identity fraud, the greater majority of fraudulent losses involves some form of identity theft. This book will both educate and allow you to take the necessary steps to ensure you do not become a victim of identity theft and fraud.

If I mention that you are not safe here anymore—and I am actually talking about your own home, businesses, and neighbourhood—please remember the world has changed, and unless *you* change, you are probably going to become a victim of white collar crime. This book will bring you the knowledge to distinguish the different types of fraudulent activity that are going on and the tools you need to protect yourself and your family.

I really want to save you a lot of thinking, so if you remember nothing else, remember this: In today's world, your personal identification is priceless, and it all has value on the street. I can sell your driver's licence for at least two hundred dollars and I might even get twenty-five dollars for your Social Insurance card.

Okay, listen up. You must safeguard and protect your identity. I mean, do you really think it's a good idea to have two of you out there? The big problem here is that if a crime is committed, we (the police) will initially come after you, because we do not realize that somebody else is out there doing a lot of crime in your name; that someone is working in your name, using your SIN number; has obtained credit cards in your name; has used your identification to rent an apartment . . . I could fill the rest of the book by just listing the crimes that are committed by bad guys. Hopefully you get the picture.

So, if you want to keep your head above water, you must protect your driver's licence, birth certificate, Social Insurance Number, health card, passport, citizenship card, and so on. Never forget that the information contained in those sources is extremely valuable to some of today's criminals. Once they have one or two of the above items, they can effortlessly "become you."

If you are not in a mall or on public transit at this point in time, take a moment right now and look in your wallet or handbag. If you are carrying more than a driver's licence, one credit card, and one debit card, you might not survive. Dramatically limit the amount of identification you carry and secure the rest. Yes, lock it up.

Get ready—here is your FIRST TIP: If you are going to protect your identification and keep some of it under lock and key, then don't just hand it over to the first person who asks for it!

Remember: *Never give out personal and financial information to unsolicited telephone callers, door-to-door solicitors, or e-mails.* Some criminals take pride in talking you out of your info, because as you already know, they do not necessarily need your actual cards; the numbers and information contained therein will suffice. You can shop on-line with your credit card numbers, but if *I* have them, I can also shop on-line with your credit card numbers. The difference here is that I am shopping somewhat free of care, because you are paying for my purchases!

As identification theft, mortgage fraud, title fraud, debit and credit card fraud, and cheque fraud keep expanding, you must become proactive. This book will assist you in protecting yourself, but you also have to do the work. Doing nothing is no longer an option. Doing nothing will eventually lead to you spending weeks, if not months, trying to get your credit and financial well being somewhat back on track.

Here is TIP #2: It is a whole lot easier to complete a little bit of daily financial maintenance than to try and repair your credit and finances after the bad guys have had their way with you.

1: THE BASICS

THEFT, FRAUD, IDENTITY THEFT, and IDENTITY FRAUD: which is which, and what is what, and should we really care? It would be difficult to spend the next few years in North America and not become a victim of one of the above or at least have a family member become a victim. The fact is that fraud, and particularly identity theft and fraud, is ever increasing. You have to protect yourself and your family, you have to know and understand what the bad guys are attempting to do to you, and how they are doing it. If you simply keep your head in the sand and adopt the position that it will never happen to you, your personal assets will almost surely start to disappear.

When we investigate identity theft and fraud offences, we spend a lot of time with the victims. They always want to know why they were targeted (the old "Why me?"). Bearing in mind that there are so many different types of frauds perpetrated on individuals that it would be impossible to give one answer, one of the common threads is the fact that in a lot of cases the victims helped—*they actually assisted*—the bad guys in defrauding them. I have really wanted to ask, why help, why give them a leg up, why tie the can to yourself, to assist them in taking your money? Okay, maybe I'm getting a little carried away, but when I explain to a victim how this happened and what he did to further the offence, how his actions gave the criminals a free pass to his money, he often reacts with language that cannot be printed in a family book. Well, something like holy ****, or please tell me I'm not that ***n dumb!

STOP helping the criminals! They're doing a great job on their own and they don't need your input. But hey, let's sink their ship before it sails away with your hard-earned money. Don't panic—read on, and I will definitely give you the 411 on what you have to do. Let me put it another way: When the criminals reach for your assets, how about we kick theirs!

Basic, No-Frills Definitions

Theft

Theft is pretty simple, not hard to understand at all. Usually when someone steals some of your property, you realize it and recognize it almost immediately. For example, you get up in the morning and walk out to the driveway to find that your car is not there; or you come home from the office and notice that your back door is open and your computer, sound system, silverware, and jewellery are missing. Theft is obviously not difficult to detect, and it is readily apparent that something is askew.

Fraud

Fraud is a lot more difficult to distinguish; it usually takes days, months, or even years to realize that it has happened. Fraud in some aspects is theft, but it is theft with a cover-up, and the cover-up is utilized to deceive and to hide the fact that theft has taken place. For example, you may purchase a used automobile privately, with ten thousand kilometres on the odometer, told that it was driven only on Sundays by a retired schoolteacher, and never in the winter, only to find out three months later that it's a stolen vehicle.

Identity Theft

Identity theft happens when someone either utilizes some of your identification for his/her own purposes or simply does anything using your name. *When someone else is you*, for example, that person could show up at a post office with photo identification containing your name and address and his/her own photo, and have your mail redirected to another location.

Identity Fraud

Now that I have acquired identification in your name, I can commit various forms of fraud and it all comes back to you. For example, I can acquire credit cards in your name, and start shopping, and it all goes on your tab.

FRAUD 101

When I was first transferred to the RCMP's Toronto Commercial Crime Section (CCS), I wasn't really sure what fraud was. Now this is not really a good thing, because my job was to investigate fraud, whatever that was. So let me help all of us out by giving a perspective on fraud that examines how it has evolved over time.

Just before I do that, I must talk about the RCMP's Toronto Commercial Crime Section. This truly was one of North America's—if not the world's—most professional police groups. The majority of the seventy members had undergraduate degrees, some with LLBs, some with accounting degrees, some with master's degrees; it truly was a great place to learn. During my ten years in this section, I was promoted to sergeant and then staff sergeant; it doesn't get any better. Believe me, I'm not bragging (okay, maybe I am a little bit)—no other police force in the world could put together a squad with that much professionalism, academic credentials, and hands-on experience; it truly was an honour to serve in Toronto CCS.

Back to the main reason we had Toronto CCS—**fraud.** Let me remind you that fraud occurs when someone attempts to acquire your money, assets, or other valuable security, and it usually involves some type of cover-up or deceptive practice that hides the actual offence until sometime in the future. Most fraud perpetrated against individuals is not detected for at least thirty days, because we never seem to use the tools that are readily available to help detect attacks on our assets.

WHY NOT? Don't just sit there worrying! Get proactive. If you wait for them to attack, you are always going to be on the losing side. Once criminals start attempting to grab your assets, they leave footprints, and if you know where to look and what to look for; you can usually shut them down before they get into full gear. Know what to look for, know what they are attempting to do and how they will likely do it, and you're probably going to survive.

THE FIFTIES

Think back to a Sunday evening at Grandma's, fifty years ago. There was Grandma sitting on the front porch with little Spots the spaniel, Grandpa was touching up the paint on the white picket fence surrounding the house, and the front door was open because Grandma never locked it. Some of the neighbours came walking by and stopped and chatted for five to ten minutes. Life was good. At this point in time, a cell phone was something they used in the local jail, the Internet was something Grandpa went fishing with, and a credit card was how Grandpa kept score in a cribbage game. (Now, of course, Grandma is locked inside the house; she never opens the door, and has it locked five different ways. Little "Spots" has been replaced by Rex the Rottweiler, she doesn't know the neighbours, and believes the house across the street is a grow-op. Grandma was a lot safer and totally fraud-proof fifty years ago.)

This was a time when no one locked the front door; a time when you knew almost everyone in your neighbourhood, and, depending on the size of the town you lived in, you probably knew or had heard of virtually everybody. When you conducted business at the local stores or companies, you knew at least one person who worked there, or you may have gone to school with the business owners or their children. Everybody knew everybody. If someone knocked on your door and indicated that he was Stanley Robins from West Brant, you actually knew, or knew of, the Robins family, and you certainly knew if this was in fact Stanley Robins.

There were no credit cards, there were no computers, no automatic teller machines, no cell phones and, lest I forget, there was virtually no fraud. In fact, if we were sitting around planning to defraud somebody, what could we do? And how were we going to do it? The people that we could target knew us, and there really were not many instruments that we could utilize to obtain their money or other assets. I should mention, though, that we always had some people, and we still have them around today, only more of them, who are selling that good old magic elixir that cured everything—yes, the good old snake oil sales-persons; they just never seem to go away.

At night, you would put your milk bottles on the front porch; they were worth five cents each, and in the morning those bottles were still there. Cigarettes were twenty-nine cents a package, pop was ten cents, and gasoline was twenty-eight cents a gallon. It probably wasn't worth attempting to defraud anybody, and it also was next to impossible. At this point in time, those who had a telephone had a party line, which meant that the neighbourhood busybody could pick up serious intelligence by listening to your telephone conversations (neighbourhood watch), but don't forget, we all knew each other, and fraudulent activity on a large scale simply was not happening.

Now, the odd time a stranger may knock at your door, but because he was a stranger, you wouldn't deal with him—unless he was from a trusted company that you had historically felt comfortable dealing with; companies like Electrolux, Encyclopedia Britannica, Tupperware, Avon, or the Fuller Brush Man; and then most of his brushes were under a dollar.

This was a time when the majority of women were housewives, and consequently there was usually someone at home. There was no opportunity to break into residences, steal mail, identification, or banking information. Even if you could break into a home and steal things, the police most likely knew who you were, which would lead to an expeditious apprehension. It is clear that the average busy housewife didn't have the time to sit down and watch TV, and even if she wanted to, she probably only had a radio. This means that there was no opportunity for criminals to see what types of crimes were committed and how they were perpetrated. No crime-stoppers re-enactments to watch, no television shows on fraud, theft, or bank scams; you simply had to do your own thinking and come up with your own plans.

Even if you could think of a good scam or scheme (at least on paper), there were very few tools that you could manipulate to defraud somebody.

It was clear that the fifties were probably a great time to be an adult, but there were limitations. Most individuals did not make a purchase until they had saved the money. If you bought anything on time, it was usually from the corner grocery store or butcher shop, and like the milkman, the bread man, and the iceman, everybody was paid on your payday. Think of it, no e-mails, no cell phones, no computers, no blackberries, no credit cards, no bank machines, no ipods, no call forwarding, no caller ID, and no Internet banking or commerce. This of course all adds up to virtually no fraud.

A lot of today's fraud involves attacking your assets at financial institutions or through products that are obtained from financial institutions. However, in the fifties the bank was a scary place for the average citizen. The branch manager probably knew every aspect of your historical financial well being, and probably knew what you required before you requested it. There were virtually no bankruptcies and people generally did what it took to meet their financial obligations. In most cases, if you were attempting to secure a mortgage, the funds were almost always held in trust by a law firm.

The bank was a great place to work, not because of the environment, but because of the hours—10:00 a.m. to 3:00 p.m., Monday to Friday. No weekends, no drive-through tellers, no twenty-four-hours-a-day cash machines; just a nice, tiny business entity that could be managed on-site and could expeditiously detect anything that appeared to be fraudulent or heading south in a rapid manner.

The biggest point I can make here is that the bank employees knew you, or they had a pretty good idea who you were. It was virtually impossible for anyone to enter the bank and pretend to be you. This is really huge. If we were still able to keep one aspect of the good old days, one thing that would keep fraudsters in their place, I would opt for bank employees' knowing with whom they are dealing; yes, this would be *numero uno* in my prevention strategy. Did someone ask how we are going to do this? It's simple: take a photo of all bank customers and download the photo into the computer system. When a client or member comes into the branch, the teller brings up the account and the first thing they see is the photo.

There were some problems in the fifties. Most restaurants closed after the dinner hour; there were no fast-food restaurants, no pizza places, no *"33 Or Free."* Think about it—no Tim

Horton's. Gosh! No Timmy's! Where the heck did the cops go for coffee? The only sort of fraud we experienced at that point in time involved things like purchasing a meal in a restaurant and not having the funds to pay for it, or acquiring lodging in a hotel without proper funds. This all occurred because you paid right after the goods or services were rendered.

And really, there just was not any time to commit fraud; you spent time wrestling with the icebox, then you had to defrost the fridge and then you had to spend a lot of time trying to get all of that frozen food into the new freezer. In some cases your wife was busy on the roof turning the TV aerial while you relaxed watching a snowy TV station. Eventually, your wife bought a pair of "rabbit ears"—the indoor antenna used then—and this of course kept her off the roof. When your wife wasn't serving as a TV technician, she was busy preparing the three meals a day that the family usually ate together; you always knew where everyone was at all times.

Neighbours were like family. They knew your business, you knew theirs, everybody communicated and always helped each other, and each new neighbour provided another set of eyes in the neighbourhood.

The point I am trying to make here is that if we could eliminate the bank and all of its products in the new millennium, we could put a lid on fraud. However, in today's world, financial institutions and every product associated with them appear to be an essential part of life. This is a long way of saying that without credit cards, debit cards, mortgages, bank accounts, cheques, lines of credit, etc., there would be little fraud, but at the same time, it would be virtually impossible to conduct everyday life as we know it today. Without a chequing account, a credit card, a debit card, a mortgage, an automated teller machine (ATM) and the Internet, we would not be able to function.

FAST-FORWARD TO TODAY

With the rolling out of credit cards, Diners Club, and Chargex, we began to see above-normal fraudulent activity that eventually exploded and has never really been controllable. At this point, if we add cheques into the mix, we now have two of the tools that are utilized at this point in time to defraud people. Now, if we add the ATM and debit card, we have four items that are still sort of the main vehicles used by many perpetrators of fraud.

Today we live in towns and cities where we do not know the majority of the people even on our street. We deal with businesses that we are not familiar with and we interact on a daily basis with individuals we have never met before. Most of us carry high-limit credit cards; most of us utilize debit cards either at automated teller machines or point-of-sale terminals. In the majority of two-parent families, both parents work. Almost everyone has a chequing account, e-mail, and a cell phone. When you put all of these basic everyday life things together, we become very susceptible to the criminal element.

For reasons that I've never really understood, many of us carry our social insurance card in our purse or wallet, and readily give our social insurance number to all who ask. We carry our birth certificate, and some of us even carry our passport. Many individuals walk around with a number of different credit cards, corporate calling cards, etc. Another little problem that we all seem to have in common revolves around what to do with the cards and identification that are not on our person. Actually, it's not really a little problem, is a *huge* problem, because we just seem to leave this stuff sitting around our residence. All of these identification faux pas lead to IDENTITY THEFT, which leads to IDENTITY FRAUD.

If you combine all of the aspects of fraud with all of the parts of identity theft, there is now an almost infinite number of ways for someone to commit both fraud and identity fraud on businesses and individuals. What makes this combination extremely dangerous to all of us is the fact that someone is committing these types of frauds using your good name, and it is very difficult—if not impossible—to apprehend some of these perpetrators. Now that they have ways and means to commit fraud and identity theft, they have reached a point where the commission of these offences becomes even easier.

With fraud and identity theft being the crime of the millennium, and increasing to a point where the number of fraudulent complaints to the police by the public at large has increased enormously, the chances of these occurrences being investigated in a timely fashion, if at all, are very slim. This coupled with the fact that the bad guys now have an amazing array of tools that they can utilize to defraud you, and the ability to perpetrate these frauds in your name, using your identification, anywhere, at any time.

Suffice it to say, this is not good. Clearly this is a recipe for disaster, because if I can commit fraud in your name with impunity, I am never going to stop. If I can make $5,000 or $10,000 every time I use your ID, do you think I am going to stop?

Does this mean that you will have to do your own investigation—sort of, "Move over, Sherlock, I'm here"? The short answer is *no*, but you do have to know what is going on, what to look for, and how to prevent the frauds from happening to you. Once the criminals get started on your assets, and you finally realize they are at your doorstep, it's too late. How many times over the years has somebody said to you, *the times they are a-changing*? Both you and I know they were right.

Everyday life as we knew it even five or ten years ago is dramatically different now, and there are a hell of a lot more criminals out there looking to tap into your assets. You might be wondering if some of their schemes will be detected, and I will say yes, but probably not until long after some of the perpetrators have left town. Are some of these bad guys going to get arrested? Maybe, but never forget: In today's world you must devote some of *your own* time to ensure that your dough is not leaving town with them.

Many people who become victims of fraud ask me if they will ever get their money back, and the short answer is *no, no,* and one more time, *noooo*. The majority of bad guys involved in fraud are judgment-proof; they have no assets, no money, and usually no place to live. The odd time I have worked on criminals who had very affluent life styles, owning condos, boats, high-end cars, vacation homes, and many toys, none of these things were in their names. This is a real problem, because they have been charged and convicted, and a criminal compensation order issued, but the money is in offshore banks, and the assets are at arm's length. This gives you one hundred percent of nothing, which you already know is a bad deal. At the very end of the day, some money may come back from the criminals, but it is usually a drop in the bucket compared to what you have lost.

A few years ago, I was investigating a fraud in the Hamilton area, and as I was driving down the bad guy's street looking for his residence, I noticed a home with a new roof, a new fence, a new porch, a new swimming pool, and two new cars in the driveway. I did not even bother to look up his house number—I knew this was my guy. This was clearly a first-time offender, with more assets than we could haul away, so if you ever get defrauded, I sure hope it's by a guy like this, because once he learns the ropes, the assets will be well hidden.

2: WHITE COLLAR CRIME:
THE PEN IS MIGHTIER
THAN THE SWORD . . .

Did you ever get up one morning and ask yourself, why fraud? I mean, is it just me, or is everybody trying to defraud everybody else? What the heck is going on? Has evil won over good, has wrong trampled on right, has bad become the victor? Does it seem that every time you pick up a newspaper or watch the news, somebody else has been defrauded, somebody else just lost his life savings, or someone just got charged with defrauding her employer? One thing is for sure: they are definitely gaining on us.

You can stop wondering. Fraud has always been around and it is never going to go away. It's like the proverbial dike: you might be able to plug it or get it temporarily stopped in one place, but before sunset it will break through somewhere else. There are so many different ways to defraud people, and so many tools that can be utilized, it just isn't possible to stop bad guys from committing fraud.

If someone is looking for fast money in a short period of time, fraud appears to be the answer. It is very lucrative, and even those individuals who get caught and are charged by the police never seem to get penalties that fit the crime. A few years ago, I was working on a stock market fraud involving two individuals who had defrauded a Mutual Fund Company of approximately thirty million dollars. Both of them were charged by the RCMP and convicted, both have now served their sentences, and one of these individuals still has fifteen million dollars.

There are many scary things about fraud; one of the scariest is the fact that almost anyone can do it. The bad guys might not always be successful, but they will always keep on trying. It's not unusual that a criminal attempting to open a number of bank accounts at six different banks will ultimately be successful; even if he is refused at one branch, he will keep on trying until he successfully opens the number of bank accounts he requires.

While you're relaxing at home reading my book, your doorbell might ring, and when you answer the door, you might have an individual standing there who claims to be representing some charitable organization or corporation. Just the other day, I answered my front door and saw a forty-five to fifty-year-old male standing there reading what appeared to be my Hydro bill. Immediately I thought that he was from Hydro, but then he asked to see my Hydro bill. Thinking that he already had it, I asked to see what he was reading, at which point he put the Hydro bill away. I then asked if he in fact was an employee of my local Hydro provider, and he indicated that he represented another electrical company. I asked him to leave my property. But as I closed the door, I marvelled at how an individual standing on my porch with one of my Hydro company's bills almost had me believing that he was an employee of my Hydro company, even though initially he never said a word.

I have probably already mentioned that fraud is never what it seems to be. Always ask some questions—or better still, don't answer the door. It's pretty amazing that I could have been defrauded by an individual who didn't really speak to me but was holding a symbol that automatically led me to believe that he was something he was not. Ouch.

EIGHTY PERCENT

Eighty percent of all frauds perpetrated on the average citizen could have been stopped before they commenced or at least discovered in the initial stages.

The eighty-percent frauds require some of our personal information, driver's licence numbers, SIN card, birth certificate, bank accounts, debit card information, credit card number, personal identification numbers (PIN), passports, etc. As previously mentioned, in a lot of cases we unwittingly give this data to the criminals, or we fail to take proper measures to protect it.

TWENTY PERCENT

The other twenty percent of frauds occur as a result of our being targeted. Some of these frauds cannot be prevented, but they can also usually be caught in the initial stages. These types of frauds may also be resolved through certain types of insurance and fraud prevention programs.

Remember, a lot of what can happen to your financial assets is directly related to your ability to protect your personal biographical information on a continuing basis. It should be noted that almost every tool that adds convenience to your life can also serve as a vehicle to obtain your personal information. As you read through this book, I have included a number of chapters on fraud prevention, including things that you can do from home to ensure that the bad guys don't get their hands on your assets.

WHITE-COLLAR CRIME (FRAUD)

I am hoping to keep this book in a very simple format, so I do not intend to write a lot about the complex legal definitions or issues surrounding fraud. However, if you are interested, what follows are the nuts and bolts of fraud without paragraph after paragraph of complex legalities.

Fraud is the art of deliberate deception for unlawful purposes. Today's criminals bring savvy and sophistication to white-collar crime. Some of them understand the banking system, the Internet, accounting practices, the stock market, and payment cards. They have been able to successfully engineer scams at all levels of society and seem to be one step ahead of everyone else. They are never going to stop trying to attack your assets; to survive, you have to be prepared. Criminals are quick to adapt; are you?

Remember that fraudulent scams and schemes are frequent, and some of the perpetrators are practised professionals (they are actors). They are persuasive, ingratiating, and able to con the most sophisticated members of society.

INHERENT ASPECTS OF FRAUD

- Some frauds are extremely simple to perpetrate. There are identity theft cases involving preteens. Shopping with your credit card or debit card is really easy.

- It is very lucrative. Most identity thieves are able to obtain at least $10,000 with your ID and thousands more if you do not catch on to the fact that they have caught up to you.

- Some of the tools required are readily available and very elementary, i.e., your mail, your garbage, and your name.

- Almost anyone can do it. Many individuals arrested in identity theft cases were from very low-level street gangs.

- There is little chance of being caught (they are using your ID). Unfortunately, it all comes back to you.

- If someone actually is caught, he or she will receive minimal fines and sentences.

- Perpetrators usually receive non-custodial sentences (to be served at home).

- Fraudsters are not deterred by the courts.

TYPES OF WHITE-COLLAR CRIMES

At this point, I am going to give you some bare-bones definitions of the types of white-collar crimes in vogue today, but do not fear—I will certainly spend more time on some of these frauds in later chapters.

- **Advance Fee Schemes**
  Any time you pay in advance for goods or services to be delivered or performed in the future, it is an advance fee scheme. This was the crime of choice of the eighties, and because these are very profitable types of crimes, they have continued to flourish and show no signs of abating. Be very, very careful any time you send money to a previously unknown person or company for goods to be delivered at

some future time. The same principle applies to anyone requiring full payment prior to performing any type of service.

- **Credit Card Fraud**
  Criminals can either apply for cards in your name, or skim your card and make a clone. Credit card fraud never seems to go away; in fact it appears to be ever expanding. You have to remember that if you are carrying a credit card with a five- or ten-thousand-dollar limit, to criminals that is five or ten thousand dollars in their pocket. One of the reasons that credit card fraud is ongoing and probably will not go away is because criminals have been extremely successful in taking that five or ten thousand dollars.

- **Debit Card Fraud**
  Criminals can skim your card, record your PIN number, and produce a clone. There was a time when the bad guys required a camera to capture your PIN number, and in some locations they still do. But keep in mind that these sophisticated criminal groups have been able to configure point-of-sale terminals so as to capture your PIN number within the terminal.

- **Financial Account Takeover**
  Criminals enter your financial institution with a piece of your identification and withdraw funds from your account. There was a time when financial institutions, brokerage houses, etc., had a "know your client rule"; in today's world, this simply is not possible. As a result, a bad guy who can produce identification in your name is able to withdraw cash from your chequing and savings accounts.

- **Cheque Fraud**
  Your personal or corporate cheques are almost the same as cash to many criminals. At this point in time, there is a tremendous problem with bad guys either depositing, or presenting for cash, altered or fictitious cheques.
  Perpetrators can acquire one of your cheques and wash the numbers and payee off of the cheque, raise the amount of the cheque, and change the payee.

- **Title Fraud**

  This is as difficult as crime gets, when you get up one morning to find that someone has fraudulently switched the title on your home, and at this point in time you no longer own it. Individuals utilizing "straw buyers" can sell your house to the straw buyers, thus changing the ownership of your home.

- **Mortgage Fraud**

  If you have a tremendous equity position in your residence, then you become a target for mortgage fraud. As previously mentioned, criminals can show up at a financial institution utilizing a piece of your identification and take out a mortgage on your property. They also can discharge your existing mortgages and then re-mortgage your home and take the funds.

- **Identification Theft**

  Through some type of theft at your home, your office, your car, or your purse or wallet, criminals can acquire pieces of your identification.

- **Theft of Your Mail**

  Someone simply comes up to your front door and removes your mail from the mailbox.

- **Investment Fraud**

  We all know somebody who invested money in either XYZ Widgets or with some friends' or relatives' enterprise that never got off the ground. Many people unsuspectingly invest with individuals who are working from shell companies that have no product, service, or purpose, other then scamming you.

- **Counterfeit Currency**

  Think about the return on your investment if you are buying goods and services with counterfeit money. I think we all agree that this crime is never going away.

  Because many companies will not accept Canadian 100-dollar bills, the counterfeiters are now utilizing 50's, 20's, 10's, and 5's.

- **Phishing**
  This is the use of e-mail and counterfeit sites that appear to be from legitimate companies but are really counterfeits, with the object of obtaining personal information from you.

- **Vishing**
  This is phishing with voice mail: you receive voice mails or are asked to call specific numbers that appear to be legitimate companies but are really fronts for criminal activity.

- **Skimming**
  This occurs when the data is removed from your debit or credit cards when you present them for payment at a card reader or point-of-sale terminal; criminals then use this data to make a clone of your cards.

FEATURES OF WHITE-COLLAR CRIME

Here are some reasons why white-collar crime is so successful — for the criminals.

- **It takes time for you to realize you are a victim.**
  It typically takes at least thirty days for a credit card issuer or financial institution to send you a statement. It may take you thirty more days to actually read it.

- **If successful, it is often repeated.**
  There are many cases where every five or six months, criminals reuse the same identification of individuals that they have historically utilized successfully.

- **The losses escalate quickly.**
  There are many occurrences where individuals have lost thirty to forty thousand dollars before they realized their identity had been taken over.

- **Mortgage fraud is usually perpetrated against those individuals who have a large equity position in their residences.**

- Do not give out your Social Insurance Number (SIN).

- Do not leave ownership or insurance in your vehicle when unattended.

- Expeditiously open and reconcile all monthly financial statements.

- Do not let your credit or debit cards out of your sight.

- Take all slips with you.

- Acquire an additional credit card for daily use with a very low limit.

- Open a separate account for your debit card and keep a minimal account balance.

- Never write down your personal identification number (PIN).

- Never use your date of birth or SIN as a PIN.

- Place only initials and surname on personal cheques.

- Lock your mailbox.

ARE YOUR ACTIONS ASSISTING THE BAD GUYS?

Your perception of the world at large can sometimes dictate the types of fraudulent activity that can be perpetrated on you.

1. Do you take steps to protect all of your information?

I have tried to make the point that if the bad guys can get your full name and your date of birth or address, they can do you some harm. This can be quite simply accomplished by just taking your mail.

2. Are you motivated by greed?

When we start investigating fraud, we quickly realize that a large number of individuals get trapped by fraud just to keep up with the Joneses. Yeah, we all want the bling and the SUV (depending on how much a litre of gas costs); we all want to be important; but we don't all start putting money into get-rich-

Anyone can search your title at an Ontario land title's office and ascertain what you actually paid for your home and view any existing mortgages.

- **Credit card fraud is usually perpetrated against those individuals who have an excellent credit history.**
  Criminals have ways to check your credit worthiness without directly utilizing the credit bureau.

If you are not properly protected, the losses can be dramatic. If you do not catch what is happening in the early stages, and you do not have certain types of insurance, the losses are usually substantial.

PREVENTATIVE MEASURES

At this point I am going to give you some ideas of things that you can check, that will tip you off if someone is starting to grab your money. I have listed these in point form here, but I have also devoted some other chapters to these preventive measures.

- Regularly check your credit history.

- Deal with a financial institution where employees know you.

- Regularly check your property title.

- Invest in title insurance and purchase identity theft insurance.

- Safeguard your mail.

- Shred.

- Protect all of your ID.

- Carry only minimal ID on your person.

- Put your passport, Social Insurance card, and birth certificate in a safety deposit box or home safe.

- Do not give biographical information to unsolicited telephone callers or e-mail solicitations.

quick schemes that are doomed to fail. Most of us realize that obtaining money by hooking up to endeavours that guarantee a return of at least five or six times our initial investment leads to sleepless nights, weight gain, and extreme anxiety, because when you invest some of your hard-earned cash in an effort to get millions from someone you don't really know, it never works out. You always seem to believe that tomorrow your money will arrive, but you and I both know that tomorrow will never come.

> **TIP#3: Remember that being somewhat bling-less is not the end of the world.**

3. Do you believe that somebody or some corporation will actually give you something for nothing, or almost nothing?

It is rather amazing how many people receive a telephone call or brochure in the mail that requires them to do almost nothing or put up only a few dollars in order to receive a gift, vacation package, or a condo in an exotic place valued at least fifty thousand dollars. If you are sitting at home right now, put the book down and start telephoning as many people as you can and make them an offer that fits the above scenario, and approximately forty percent of the individuals you contact will send some money. Something for nothing has been used as bait for years and will continue to be used, because so many people are willing to put up fifty dollars to get fifty thousand. If you remember very little of what you have read so far, keep this in mind: I have never met anyone up to this point in time who ever received that big-league fifty-thousand-dollar item. It just doesn't happen.

But many individuals still get involved in schemes that appear on the surface to offer extreme monetary rewards or goods for virtually nothing. At some point, these schemes require you to send money to some location, even if the money is an insignificant amount. The bad guys now have a copy of your personal cheque, the name of your bank, and your account number.

Tomorrow it may happen that you can acquire a home, a car, a vacation property, or a million dollars in cash for an outlay of ten or fifteen dollars, but up to this point in time, no one has ever received these rewards for buying twenty pens or other articles that must be purchased at a minimal cost. Acquiring something for nothing sure as heck sounds great, but even though I am an optimist, it doesn't matter—it isn't happening. Every fraud investigator in every police department in North America learns the same thing his/her first week in the fraud unit: if it seems too good to be true it probably is. Their second week in the fraud squad, they learn that **if it seems too good to be true, it's a** SCAM!

The third week in the fraud squad, they are just too busy investigating frauds to even think.

Remember, you cannot always prevent fraud from happening, but you can reduce its effects on your assets and your future lending or buying potential if you take proper steps to detect and combat it.

Fraud by its very nature is subtle. In its initial phases, you may not be aware that something is happening. But if you have taken preventive measures, acquired certain types of insurance, bought into some types of fraud prevention programs, and regularly exercise due diligence with your personal monthly accounts, its effects **will be minimal**!

Do not give out personal or financial information, no matter how urgent the caller or e-mail seems to be. Financial institutions already know your account numbers and your mother's maiden name. They will never ask you for your PIN, or for any of your money! If someone calls indicating they are the police and are attempting to acquire financial information **do not** give this information over the telephone. The police will not ask you for your PIN, for money, or for financial account information.

Do not panic when dealing with people you do not know; just hang up and call the individuals and companies you normally deal with. Scare tactics are often utilized by criminals seeking personal or financial information. JUST HANG UP. If you want to call someone, use the telephone numbers on the back of your credit cards, or on your monthly statements.

3: IDENTITY THEFT

IDENTITY THEFT AND FRAUD

Heads up! If at this point in the book you do not recognize that identity theft and fraud are lurking just around the corner, and could eventually catch up to you; if you don't realize that you must learn the 411 on this stuff, then warm up the milk, have another cup of tea, and then go to bed. But hey, yes, I'm sure that you already know that this stuff is very, very, bad and I know you are ready to continue.

OKAY, STOP RIGHT HERE, take a short break, but just for a minute, put your feet up, take a deep breath, put the Leafs on for a couple of seconds, just to clear your head. Now, let's be honest: some of you just skimmed the first few pages, didn't really read all of the paragraphs. Yes, I know you're busy, but listen up: this is extremely important. If you can live long enough and you never learn about identity theft and fraud, they will eventually bite you in the pocketbook. This is where it's at, this is what is happening right now, this is your world that you interact with daily, and yes, it is fraught with a huge bunch of criminals trying to obtain and utilize your ID.

We have all been in relationships where at some point somebody (hopefully a *fox* or a *hunk*) looked over at you and said, oh, oh, oh, honey, there should be two of you! Well, you know what? In today's world they get their wish. While you're sitting there telling your significant other how great he/she is, some crook is probably out there telling some bank employee how great she/he is for arranging a new mortgage in your good name. Ouch! Relax, but don't put the Leafs back on, you don't want to freak out; just sit back, read carefully, and make sure you *comprende* this chapter, *comprende*?

I am just sitting here reading the Saturday *Sun*. I have put the book down for a while because I've already read it twice this week, and that's enough until next week. Now the *Sun* has yet another headline—almost the same headline that I see every time I open the paper to something other than the sunshine girl—where the police have arrested yet another gang that has been placing devices and cameras on ATMs. Does this never get old; do you the public still not understand what is going on? Almost every time I open the paper, there is another headline about bad guys using ATM tampering devices. This of course results in bad guys skimming your ATM card and then cloning it and using it to withdraw money from your account at an ATM or at point-of-sale terminals.

Yes, this is another form of identity theft. These people are walking around with either a clone of your card or a counterfeit card in your name. Come on! How many times do the police have to arrest skimmers before you realize that this is a major problem and decide to protect yourself?

When you finish reading this book, you will be able to immediately recognize card skimmers or the fact that you are missing money from your account. Let's get ATM fraud STOPPED in its initial phase; it has been going on far too long and it is one of the easier frauds to detect.

I have always been amazed at how simple it is to perpetrate identity theft; the tools required are readily available, and many of the individuals involved in this type of crime have limited academic credentials, and in some cases, even limited English language skills. You must understand that identity theft is virtually unstoppable, and many of the perpetrators are never detected, because they are using *your* identification, and it all comes back to *you*.

Just imagine you have just been promoted, given the Gold Shield, and assigned to the Fraud Squad. First day on the new job, the staff sergeant calls you in to his or her office, gives you the good old "welcome aboard," and hands you fifty identity fraud files. Okay, don't look at me, what are you going to do? Where the heck do you start? You've got fifty files there, detective, that YOU have to investigate, not me! You can see the problem: you are holding fifty complaints to the police from at least fifty people who claim that somebody has taken their money. Problem is, when you read through the files, the money was either taken by them, or by somebody who *said* they were them. Which is it? Welcome to the world of IDENTITY FRAUD. Oh yes—and if it wasn't them, who was it?

IDENTITY THEFT
(WHEN SOMEONE ELSE IS YOU)

MUCH OF TODAY'S WHITE-COLLAR FRAUD IS DIRECTLY LINKED TO ID THEFT.

This is the fastest-growing white-collar crime in Canada and the rest of the world. It is a gateway for a number of other fraudulent activities that are directly related to the unauthorized use of your identity. You might ask yourself the following question: Self, who the heck are we dealing with? Did we just give some of our money to someone we believe to be Rachel So-and-So? She showed us ID, but was that really hers? Did she really represent the company she said she worked with? Did we make a mistake? Can we get our money back?

Welcome to the new millennium, where identity theft and fraud are a fact of life! This problem is not going to go away, so you have to get involved in understanding it and detecting it.

Identity theft occurs when criminals use your personal identification without your knowledge or consent to commit crimes such as fraud or theft. Perpetrators steal key pieces of your personal identification, or acquire identification in your name, and then use it to impersonate you and commit crimes in your name.

Thieves can also simply target you and obtain identification in your name. They do this by altering legitimate identification (resulting in a "genuine altered ID") or creating counterfeit or fictitious identification in your name.

I cannot emphasize enough that identity thieves/criminals are everywhere and they spend almost every waking hour attempting to obtain biographical information on you. If they are not able to steal some of your identification, they can obtain your name through the Ministry of Transportation, providing they have the licence plate number from your car. They can also show up at any land/title office and obtain the full name or names of all those who are on title at your residence. If they do not wish to travel too far, as previously mentioned they can simply remove (steal) the mail from your mailbox and obtain your bank and credit card statements.

THIEVES ATTEMPT TO OBTAIN YOUR:

Full name
Complete address
Telephone number
Social Insurance number
Driver's licence number
Credit card and banking information
Bank cards
Calling or business cards
Birth certificate
Passport
Financial statements

Can you imagine what I could do to you, even if I had only three of the above items? It reminds me of a friend of mine who was an investigator with one of the federal agencies. One day he received a telephone call from an elderly Jamaican male, who said that he had married the wrong woman! Now please bear in mind that this is serious business, no smirking—hey, is he the only married man to ever utter that statement? All right, you and I know that many wives have also made a similar call, probably to their shrink . . . but back to our friendly Jamaican. He told my friend that he had met and married a younger Jamaican woman. Now, this sounds like a great deal to me, particularly because the caller was retired. You might ask yourself, what's the problem?

For a start, when the bride went back home for a month's holiday, her new husband went through her belongings and discovered that she had over a hundred Social Insurance cards in her dresser drawer. Then he saw that the name on one of the cards was the name she had used when they married. Turns out our blushing bride was a nurse's aide at two nursing homes, and had been helping the patients and also helping herself.

Note: When you have a friend or a relative in a hospital or nursing home, make sure that you take all of their ID, credit cards, debit cards, payment cards, and any cash they might have with them and keep this stuff offsite.

YOUR IDENTITY DOCUMENTS CAN BE OBTAINED IN THE FOLLOWING WAYS:

- **Stealing mail from your residential mail box**.
  It is imperative that you do not leave mail overnight in a residential mailbox, be it at your home, in a Canada Post super box, or in an apartment or condominium mailroom.

- **Redirecting your mail at the post office.**
  As long as we have had crime and criminals, one of the oldest tools utilized by this group of individuals is the redirecting of your mail. These individuals go to a post office and have your mail sent to a post office box; to disguise the fact that it's a post office box, they use the word "suite." For example, if the new address is P.O. Box 6305, 2001 Main Street East, this address now becomes 2001 Main Street East, Suite 6305.

- **Stealing identification from your wallet, purse, motor vehicle, home, or office; or even by tracking e-mails you've sent or Web sites you have visited.**
  All identification not on your person should be secured, either in a safe in your home or in a safety deposit box. There is no reason to carry your passport unless you are travelling, and there is absolutely no reason to be carrying your SIN card or birth certificate on your person.
  There are many stories about bad guys stealing identification, but I love the ones that have happened in some of the office towers in most of Canada's larger

cities. Most managers, vice presidents, etc., have their own offices, so it is not unusual for them to leave their handbag, wallet, jacket, or sweater in their office if they are somewhere else for only a few minutes. Now think about this: who is the one person who could enter these offices without the secretary's getting suspicious or stopping him? Hey, hey, come on, don't just read on—think about it for a couple of seconds!

Yes, anyone dressed like a maintenance person carrying a wrench or a paintbrush. You just have to know that three or four times a year, offices are ransacked and identification stolen, and the only person anyone can think of on the floor was a painter, or at least someone they perceived to be a painter because he was carrying a paintbrush!

- **Purchasing confidential information from government employees, personnel at financial institutions, those working in credit bureaus, or anyone working where personal or financial information is stored.**
  Unfortunately, many individuals working for minimum wage, or those who are simply greedy, seem to be easily persuaded into stealing information from their employers. A good example of this is clerks who are working in gas bars and will skim credit cards for a fee of ten or fifteen dollars per card.

- **Sourcing or researching public documents, e.g., newspapers, telephone books, libraries, and all government records in the public domain.**
  If you have some free time, go to any major public library and simply conduct research on yourself in the "old newspaper" area; you will be amazed at the information you might find on yourself, your family, or your employer.

- **Stealing your garbage (on garbage day at your residence, or any day at business dumpsters). Shred, Shred, Shred!** If you are operating a business, you *must* shred.

- **Extracting information from applications that you completed for employment, housing, or credit, and believed to be legitimate, not knowing that they were offered by bogus entities.** There are many stories involving individuals who attended trade shows, conferences, or conventions and filled out applications for credit cards, and then had their identification taken over. One of two things happened: either the individuals that they interacted with were not legitimate, or the information on the application was not properly protected.

ONCE THEY HAVE YOUR IDENTIFICATION, THEY CAN DO THE FOLLOWING:

- Redirect your mail

- Apply for a credit card in your name

- Open financial accounts in your name

- Apply for an ATM card in your name

- Apply for loans in your name

- Apply for a line of credit in your name

- Apply for a mortgage in your name

- Change the title on your home

- Obtain employment with your SIN

- Collapse your RRSP

- Obtain a power of attorney over you

Any of the above can happen when someone goes into a financial institution or a lawyer's office with a photo ID in *your* name, with *their* photo.

Remember: with your identification, they can become you and they can now do almost anything that you can do.

One of the earliest identity theft cases I became involved with happened in the early '90s, when I was investigating a significant financial loss in a department of a corporation. When I commenced the investigation, it became apparent that the department manager had authorized a number of suspicious transactions. The first sign that something was amiss was when I talked to her secretary, who informed me that the manager's mother called her every day and asked for her by a name different than the one she was using.

When I went to see the individual at her condo, I told the concierge the name of the person I was looking for, and he indicated that there was no one there by that name, but there was someone with the same last name and a different first name.

It turned out that the manager had limited expertise in the area she was managing; however, she had a sister who had spent some years working in a similar area. As a result, she applied for this management job utilizing her sister's ID and resume. She was able to work in the department without drawing too much attention or suspicion, because she was in constant contact with her sister for guidance. This allowed her to manage the department's day-to-day activities. In the end, this is when identity theft leads to a significant fraudulent loss.

ADDITIONAL MEASURES FOR SELF-PROTECTION:

- Review your monthly statements from credit unions, banks, and credit card companies and report any discrepancies immediately.

- Every three to six months, get a copy of your credit report from one of the two national credit reporting agencies, Equifax Canada or TransUnion Canada.

- If your mail doesn't arrive, or if the volume of mail is dramatically reduced, contact Canada Post to ensure that your mail is not being redirected.

- If you have applied for a new credit card that hasn't arrived in a timely fashion, call the credit grantor immediately.

- If you are going to be away from home, ask a trusted neighbour to pick up your mail, or go to your local post office (with identification) and ask for Canada Post's "hold mail" service.

- Never carry your social insurance card or birth certificate on your person.

- Consider opening a credit union or bank account with a maximum balance of $500 and attach your member card (debit card) to this account. (IT SHOULD BE NOTED THAT THIS ACCOUNT SHOULD NOT HAVE A LINE OF CREDIT OR OVERDRAFT PROTECTION ATTACHED TO IT.)

- Consider obtaining a credit card with a maximum limit of $500 for everyday use.

- Rent a safety deposit box for all documents and valuables that need to be safeguarded from identity theft.

- Replace your existing residential mailbox with one that locks.

Most financial institutions allow their clients to utilize Internet banking. At this point in time, I'm not sure how secure Internet banking is, but I do believe that most individuals should sign on for Internet banking for one primary reason: to give individuals the ability to monitor, on a real-time daily basis, all debits and credits to their personal accounts. This gives you the ability to immediately recognize debits to your chequing or savings accounts that you have not authorized.

THE FOLLOWING ARE SIGNS THAT YOUR IDENTITY MIGHT HAVE BEEN STOLEN:

- A dramatic reduction in your daily mail volume; you may not be receiving bills, monthly statements, or other regular mail, which may indicate that someone has changed the mailing address.

- Collection agencies may contact you regarding a delinquent account you did not apply for. Someone may have opened a new account in your name, or made changes to an account without your knowledge or permission.

- You discover activity in any of your financial accounts that you did not complete or authorize. A creditor calls to say you've been approved or denied credit that you haven't applied for; or you get credit card statements for accounts you don't have.

- You apply for a credit card or other form of credit and are turned down, knowing that historically you have never had any credit problems.

IF YOU ARE A VICTIM

If you are a victim, act immediately to minimize damage and help prevent further fraud or theft. When contacting various agencies, keep a written log of time and date called, the individual you spoke with, their direct line or extension, and their title. Maintain a written record of the details of the conversation.

Step One
Contact Canada's two national credit reporting agencies, TransUnion Canada and Equifax Canada.

Step Two
Contact each financial institution, credit card issuer, or other company that provided the identity thief with unauthorized credit, money, goods, or services in your name.

Step Three
Report the incident to your local police, request a copy of the report, and include it in all correspondence with financial institutions, credit issuers, credit reporting agencies, and other companies. Obtain the occurrence number that the police have assigned to your complaint.

Step Four
Report the incident to PhoneBusters National Call Centre, toll free at 1–888–495–8501.

Step Five
If your credit cards or government-issued documents have been lost or stolen, notify the issuer immediately to have the documents cancelled and new ones issued. Visit the Lost Wallet site at

www.gc.on.ca to connect to key document issuers in the provincial and federal governments and click on the "lost wallet" icon.

REMEMBER, ID FRAUD CAN HAPPEN IF:

- You are not checking the title on your residence. You must periodically ensure that the title on your residence has not been changed or altered.

- You do not have title insurance. Remember, if your title has been changed or altered, no matter what current legislation is in place, it could still cost you several thousand dollars in legal fees to have your title reinstated. In most civil cases, legal costs are awarded; however, if the perpetrator is never found, because he or she was using your identity, there is no one to obtain costs from. Title insurance will defend your title and cover most legal fees associated with reinstating your original title.

- You have not developed a personal relationship with the credit bureau. You must periodically check your credit history.

- You are not checking your monthly statements. You must expeditiously audit your statements.

- You are not shredding your personal or financial documents. Shred, Shred, Shred!

- You are not locking your mailbox. Never use a residential mailbox that does not lock.

- You do not have a safety deposit box. Documents that you do not require on a daily or weekly basis should be secured, e.g. passports, birth certificates, and SIN cards.

- You are carrying too much ID. If your wallet or purse is stolen, is there enough ID present for the perpetrator to become you?

- You give out personal information over the telephone and Internet. Do not respond or reply to unsolicited emails or telephone calls.

Yes, you have finished the chapter on identity theft and fraud, and now you know that this is the new crime wave. Really, can it get any better for the crooks? They can use your identification and start taking your money without your knowing it—or at least not until some time after the offence was committed. In such a case, you realize that something is not quite right, and (this is the best part) in most cases, nobody has a clue as to who did this. It really does not get any easier for the bad guys. Do the checks, do your financial homework, walk the walk, don't just do the talk, get these criminals away from you, and keep them away. Believe me, you can outsmart them, by being one step ahead.

Remember, this type of crime is not going to go away; but the good news is, it is easy to detect. However, you've got to keep doing the work.

Okay, this is TIP#4: Check all of your accounts and credit and debit card transactions through Internet banking and check your credit history periodically through one of the credit bureaus.

To be safe, you—yes, I am talking to you—have to do the work; no excuses—this only takes a minute per day of your time.

4: The Internet

Right now it might be 2009, or it could be 2010 when you read this book. Regardless, I hope you consider the Internet to be an integral part of your life. I say that because the Internet brings the whole world to your kitchen, living room or bedroom—wherever you have your computer. What? No computer? Please, if I can operate a computer, you sure as heck can—don't forget, I am a cop!

You can literally do anything on a computer that you can do outside your home. One of the best things is that you can communicate with family members and friends all over the world; you can instantly see pictures they have taken and share your pics with them. You can visit the world, or your own town or city, and never leave the kitchen table. And oh, yes, there are all kinds of great games you can play, some of which you can play against opponents from around the world. No more excuses! Check out the various Internet providers and then sign up. No matter what you think, your own world will be a more enjoyable and more interesting place to be, with a computer hooked up to the Internet.

Computers . . . I recall a time in 1981, the staff sergeant walked into the fraud unit and placed a file on my desk, and then walked to the door, turned around, and said, "Terry, I want you to look after that file yourself, because it is our first computer file." All of us members looked at each other and said, what the ***n is a computer? One of the constables said that he thought it was something like a filing cabinet, but instead of opening a drawer and looking for a file, you just type the name of the file in the computer, and the file automatically comes up. It sure sounded great, but we did not have a computer to try it on, so we remained skeptical. In hindsight, I now realize this constable was a lot sharper than he looked. Oh, did I mention that the perpetrator of this particular computer fraud was a fifteen-year-old male? Ouch!

Okay; stand back a bit, take a couple of deep breaths, count to ten (not out loud). We do have to talk about this Internet thing. Yeah, I know, there are some things better left unsaid, but this is not one of them. You need to know what is out there. When the world comes to your door via the 'net, it also brings danger, because along with all of the good people come the fraudsters, the scammers, the sickoooos, the pedophiles, and many, many other bad people.

> TIP #5: **When you get up in the morning and go to check your e-mail, you might find some mail that is unsolicited from people or companies you may or may not know. *Just delete it.* Do not act on it or be persuaded by it; just delete, delete, and delete.**

Believe me, the good things about the 'net far outweigh the bad stuff, but like society at large, a small percentage of people on the 'net are criminals and they are going to set traps for you. But together we can outsmart them.

Remember, the Internet is a double-edged sword. On the one hand, it can protect you, make your life easier, and make you a more social being. But it can also do you in and seduce you into sending your money or personal information to people with whom you would normally *never* deal in person.

One of the main components of the Internet is e-mail, by means of which you can communicate with people all over the world, as long as you have their e-mail address. At the same time, obviously people all over the world can send *you* mail if they have your e-mail address. And yes, this is a bit of a problem, because it allows both the good and bad people out there access to you, and they can basically send you anything they want.

For example, on their Web site, the RCMP mention West African fraud, and more specifically they mention the Nigerian/

West African letter. This letter goes back to the eighties, when individuals, usually posing as government officials, contacted thousands of people in North America and offered them an opportunity to share millions of US dollars. Okay, I know what you're thinking: Does it get any better than this—somebody you never heard of before wants to just up and give you five or ten million US. Is this a good thing? Sure *sounds* pretty good, and we've got nothing to lose, have we? HELLO, this is your wakeup call! Stop dreaming. Nobody is going to give millions of US dollars to somebody they do not know, are they? (*Fraud for Dummies* is my next book.) Just so there is no confusion, the answer is . . . wait for it . . . NOOOO!

Now what is the other side of the coin? Do you think that anybody took them up on their offer and made an attempt to get their hands on this money? Pardon, do you remember our little talk about something for nothing? Yes, if you offer anyone who hasn't read this book a flat-screen television if he/she will buy twenty pens for $21.53, you will be swamped; you'll need another savings account. Now offer the masses one, two, or three million dollars, and you will be overwhelmed, almost crushed by the landslide of responses.

Believe it or not, thousands of Canadians and Americans made contact in an effort to get that dough offered by the Nigerian Letter. Did anybody get the two or three million? Do you want me to answer the three-million-dollar question? Okay, may I have the envelope, please? What the heck, it's empty, and so are many of the bank accounts of those individuals who tried day after day to obtain all those millions. In fact, the United States Secret Service, which investigates these types of frauds in the US, believes that in the eighties and early nineties, Americans sent billions of dollars in an attempt to get their hands on the free millions being offered.

Let's change hats again. I'm going to give you your investigator's badge and place you on the Nigerian Letter Squad. Monday morning, the sergeant gives you a desk, a PC—sorry, a police cruiser—, two new notebooks, one shiny new RCMP pen, some writing paper, a bunch of forms that you must fill out daily, an old briefcase, and a handshake. Oh, I almost forgot, and thirty new files related to West African Letter Fraud. Hopefully, he also wishes you good luck, because partner, you are going to need it. You have to knock on some doors and get somebody to admit that he was silly enough to think that a person whom he had never met, who does not know him, who selected him at random, is actually going to send him five, ten, twenty, thirty, or forty million to place in his own bank account in Canada. No wonder some cops drink.

As technology and the world evolve, so do the criminals. Yes, they still send some letters, but they send a lot more e-mails; it's cheaper and faster. Basically the first type you should be aware of involves somebody trying to give you several million US to keep in your bank account in your own country. The idea here is that if you put their millions into your bank account, then they will give you a percentage of the total just for being a good person. *Who knew—where do I sign up?* Relax, let me continue. These e-mails usually involve somebody's dying, and somebody else's discovering that the dead person had millions of US dollars in a bank account in a foreign country. Yes, they want to send all of the money to you, even though they do not know you.

At this point, I am going to let you read some of the e-mails that I have gathered from the 'net. You will note that these e-mails all have the same common theme.[1]

■ ■ ■

Hi,

My name is Joy Moses and I am 19 yrs old. My mother was an African American while my father was from the french speaking colony of Cote D' Ivoire in WestAfrica, I was living with my mother not too far from Charleston building, 601 57th Street, Charleston WestVirginia USA. And i attended Charleston senior High School, 1201 Washington Street E, Charleston, WV.i lost my mother sometimes ago and after her death i came to meet my father for the very first time in Cote d' Ivoire, though he

---

1   We have left all the e-mails in this book in their original condition. You will notice that there are lots of spelling, punctuation, and grammatical errors; this alone should alert a potential victim.

was also living in the state before he relocated back to Cote d' Ivoire to set up a business.

Exactely two months and one week after i came to meet my father with the help of US consulates he died, he was very sick when i came to meet him.

But before his death, there were some document he gave to me and he told me that everything he worked for in his life time is in the documents and when I crosscheck the documents, I discovered that my late father deposited the sum of 8, Million United State dollars ($8.000.000) in a bank here in Cote D'Ivoire and he deposited the money on behalf of his foreign business partner for a security purpose though he did not mention his partner's name on the documents but, according to the agreement he made with the bank, his foreign partner is the one to claim this money as the next of kin.

What I am telling you is that I am just a young girl and there is little or nothing I could do on my own and again if my late father relative find out that my late father left that kind of money in the bank and that I have the documents with me, I don't know what they might do to me so, I need you to help me contact the bank here and claim the money for me as my late father's foreign partner and the beneficiary of the money and take me along with you.

If you do this for me apart from the love I will also offer you 5% of the total money for helping me. Please I requested for your trust and understanding because it might sound unbeleivable but it is the truth. Please get back to me as soon as posible.

Sincerely,

∎ ∎ ∎

Greetings,

I am Barr. Charles Brown, the personal attorney to late Mr Mark Michelle, a French National.

On 3rd January 2001, Mr Mark Michelle and his wife with their three children were involved in an auto crash, all occupants of the vehicle unfortunately lost their lives. Since then, I have made several inquiry with his country's embassy to locate any of his extended relatives, this has proved unsuccessful. I decided to personally contact you with this business partnership proposal to assist me in repatriating a huge amount of money left behind by my client before they get confiscated or declared non-serviceable by the finance house where this huge deposit was lodged.

The deceased had a deposit valued presently at $18,000,000.00 (Eighteen Million United States Dollars) and the bank has issued me a notice to provide his next of kin or beneficiary by will otherwise have the account confiscated. Having been unsuccessful in communicating any of my late client relatives for over two (2) years now, I am now seeking your consent to present you as the next of kin/beneficiary to the deceased so that the proceeds of this account valued at $18 Million US Dollars can be paid to you.

Already, I have worked out modalities for achieving my aim of appointing a next of kin as well as transfer the money abroad for us to share in the ratio of 50% for me and 35% to you and we shall collectively donate 10% to the Tsunami relief course while 5% will be set aside for any incurable expenses both local and international.

Your urgent response will be highly anticipated and appreciated.

Best wishes,
Barr Charles Brown

■ ■ ■

Dear,
I am contacting you right from Essex London, United Kingdom with reason that we are going to be of a great use to each other. My name is Prince George Williams, I am the first son of Late Mr.Funsho Williams. Untill his death, my father was the a governorship aspirant on the platform

of the Peoples Democratic Party (PDP) of my country (Nigeria) Fore more information about is death view:

Before I go into further details please be informed that I am writing without any other person's pre-knowledge of my contacting you, Therefore I will appreciate same attitude to be maintained all through days before the death of my father he revealed to me about a deposit of a trunk box which he deposted with my name in a Bank located in West Africa (Lagos Nigeria) for security reasons, although he registered the contents as precious stones but the real content of these trunk box is the sum of USD$18M (Eighteen Million United States of American Dollars) which was his share from a secret sale of Diamond when he was in the office.

After the burial of my father, I made frantic effort on the best way to handle this money. I sought advice from an attorney who advised that I must seek for a trustworthy foreign business partner. However, I sincerely ask for your assistance to get this Funds out of this country, and your share for assisting us will be 40% of the total sum, and the remaining 60% that will be for me and my family.

The consignment will be released within seven 7 days of my being in receipt of your reply via my alternative e-mail address prince_williams_ and I want to assure you that this transaction is 100% risk free. In case you have any question do not hesitate to contact me as I wait for your swift and favourable response to my email Or Call me direct on [phone number].

Best Regards
Prince George Williams.

∎ ∎ ∎

With Due Respect,

This is a personal email directed to you and I request that it should be treated as such. I am Barrister Dennis Plat, a solicitor at law.

My late client who worked as an independent oil magnate died in an auto-crash with his immediate family on the 5th day of Nov 2000. Since the death of my client in Nov, 2000, I have written several letters to the embassy with intent to locate any of his extended relatives whom shall be claimants/beneficiaries of his abandoned personal estate and all such efforts have been to no avail.

More so, I have received official letters in the last few weeks suggesting a likely proceeding for confiscation of his abandoned personal assets in line with existing laws by the finance and security company in which my client deposited a consignment trunk box containing the sum of $9.8m USD as family valuable. With all effort to claim this consignment box containing 9.8m USD my self has proved futile, the board of directors of the company now adopted a resolution and I was mandated to provide his next of kin for the handing over of this consignment box within the next 15 official working days or forfeit it as abandoned property.

The company had planned to invoke the abandoned property Decree of 1996 to confiscate the funds after the expiration of the period given to me but after an investigation in the finance/security company I found out that some members of the company wants to divert this fund into their private accounts for their own selfish interest and only want to use the excuse that since I am not able to look for some one to make the claim, the consignment should be made unserviceable and that means submitting the fund to the government of this country and some to the company management which is not their main intentions.

However, to forestall a total lose, I decided to search for a credible person and finding that you bear a similar last name, I was urged to contact you, that I may, with your consent, present you to the security company as my late client's surviving family member so as to enable you put up a claim to the company in that capacity as a next of kin of my client, so that the proceeds of This deposit can be given to you, before they get confiscated or declared as unserviceable to the security company where it is lodged.

I have reasoned very professionally and I know it will be legally proper to present you as the next of kin of my deceased client and this would be done in accordance with the laws of the land. This is simple, I will like you to confirm immediately your full legal names, address and date of birth so that I will prepare the necessary documents and affidavits that will put you in place as the next of kin.

Note that this is legal and 100% risk free since I have all vital documents that would be requested by them and that would confer you the legal right to make this claim. I find this possible for the main reason that you bear a similar last name with my client making it a lot easier for you to put up a claim in that capacity. Therefore, to facilitate the immediate reprofiling of this fund, you need, first to contact me via my alternative email address signifying your interest and as soon as I obtain your confidence, I will immediately intimate you with the complete details, with which you are to proceed and I shall direct you on how to put up an application to the finance and security company.

However, you will have to assent to an express agreement which I will forward to you in order to bind us in this transaction. Upon your response, I shall then provide you with more details and relevant documents that will help you understand the transaction. Please send me your confidential telephone and fax numbers for easy communication.

Please observe utmost confidentiality, let me have your opinion as soon as possible and if this proposal is acceptable by you, do not take undue advantage of the trust I have bestowed in you, I await your urgent response.

Awaiting your urgent reply via my email: dennis_plat

Sincerely,
Dennis Plat (Esq.)

■ ■ ■

PLEASE I NEED YOUR URGENT ASSISTANCE

Dear

   I am Paul Fred, from Democratic Republic of Congo. we lost our Dad and mum a couple of months ago. our Father was a serving director of the Copper and Diamonds exporting board until his death. He was assassinated along side with our mother by the rebels following the political uprising in our country. Before his death he deposited the sum of US$21.8 twenty one Million eight hundred Thousand United States dollars here in a bank here in Cote D'Ivoire which was for the importation of hydroelectric and petroleum processing machine for the establishment of his own company.

   I am contacting you to seek your good sistance to stand as our late father's bussiness partner to enable the bank transfer this money into your account in your country and you will help us to invest it into a very lucrative bussiness which you will direct us.

   As i do not have any knowledge of investment that is why we are asking for your guidence in this trancation. As our father had informed the bank that the money belonged to his oversea associate but did not mention any name to them. Please if you are willing to assist me and my sister, indicate your interest in replying back. We are ready to give you a substantial amount, like 15% of the total money as your commission for the assistance. Please your are free to ask question where ever you do not undestand very well.

   Thanks and best regards.
   From Paul Fred

∎ ∎ ∎

Subject: Urgently important

Dear Sir/Madam,
Definitely, this letter will come as a big surprise to you or perhaps startling as such business propositions does not

come to your attention on a regular basis. Also the fact that you do not know me or have met with me before.

Conscious of the value of time, I will go directly to details, thus pardon the directness of this letter. To introduce myself, I am Francis Panou, the only son and 1st of 2 offspring's of my late father Christopher Koffi Panou, Ex Prime Minister of the Togolese Republic, deceased on the 17th October 2003.

Shortly before my father's death, on his sick bed he disclosed to me highly confidential details concerning a deposit he made with a security company of 2 trunk cases containing the sum of Forty Five Million USD (US$45,000,000.00). He informed me that the funds originated from a kickback given by a Danish Oil Exploration firm for Turn around Maintenance (TAM) services of the Togolese refineries for a 10yr period during his tenure as Director, Financial Consultancy Advisory Committee to the Presidency, 1990-2000. His job specifications included identifying and contracting competent foreign firms for approved contract jobs in both the upstream and downstream sector of the oil industry.

My predicament lies on the fact that due to prevailing circumstances, I can not openly lay claim to this funds as I have just finished my studies and in order to prevent misuse of the funds my father made the deposit with firm instructions, indicating a foreign beneficiary. It is on this basis that he advised me to solicit the mutual assistance of a foreigner for the evacuation and subsequent investment of these funds abroad.

Furthermore the downward trend of economies of West African states and unstable socio-political climate prompted my decision to contact you including your impressive business profile I obtained in all confidentiality in a business journal.

Rest assured that you will be rewarded satisfactorily for your mutual co-operation but your compensation including further details will only be discussed upon your acceptance of this offer.

I urge your prompt reply to this letter which will indeed be a relief from the pain of anxiety in this most urgent matter.

Yours respectfully,
Martins Panou.

■ ■ ■

GOOD DAY TO YOU

30/10/2007

MY NAME IS MR. EDWARD MENDRIDS. I AM THE MANAGER OF THE INTERNATIONAL COMMERCIAL BANK PLC, ADIDOGOME BRANCH LOME TOGO. I AM MARRIED WITH TWO KIDS.

I AM WRITING TO SOLICIT YOUR ASSISTANCE IN THE TRANSFER OF $4,800.000.00.THIS FUND IS THE EXCESS OF WHAT MY BRANCH IN WHICH I AM THE MANAGER MADE AS PROFIT DURING THE LAST YEAR.

I HAVE ALREADY SUBMITTED AN APPROVED END OF THE YEAR REPORT FOR THE YEAR 2006 TO MY HEAD OFFICE HERE IN TOGO AND THEY WILL NEVER KNOW OF THIS EXCESS. I HAVE SINCE THEN, PLACED THIS AMOUNT OF $4,800.000.00 ON A SUSPENCE ACCOUNT WITHOUT A BENEFICIARY.

AS AN OFFICER OF THE BANK, I CANNOT BE DIRECTLY CONNECTED TO THIS MONEY THUS I AM IMPELLED TO REQUEST FOR YOUR ASSISTANCE TO RECEIVE THIS MONEY INTO YOUR BANK ACCOUNT.

I INTEND TO PART 40% OF THIS FUND TO YOU WHILE 60% SHALL BE FOR ME. I DO NEED TO STRESS THAT THERE ARE PRACTICALLY NO RISK INVOLVED IN THIS. IT'S GOING TO BE A BANK-TO-BANK TRANSFER. ALL I NEED FROM YOU IS TO STAND AS THE ORIGINAL DEPOSITOR OF THIS FUND.

IF YOU ACCEPT THIS OFFER, I WILL APPRECIATE YOUR TIMELY RESPONSE .

WITH REGARDS,
MR EDWARD MENDRIDS.

■ ■ ■

Greetings,

I am asking for your assistance to claim this inheritance fund belonging to my late client (Name Withheld) before the bank will confiscate the funds. A foreign expatriate died of overdose on Friday the 15Th of February, 2008 after taking some of his usual drug "CASODEX" .This drug is used for cancer treatments because he has been a cancer patient for over 9 years. He had US$7,000,000 in his domiciliary account with an oil firm (NNPC) here in Africa. Since his death, the fund has been unclaimed because i have not been able to locate any of his relatives abroad, and now the oil firm and the government have been contacting me as his attorney here in Nigeria, and they are also threatening to confiscate the fund if i do not present someone as beneficiary.

Please, if you are interested, sincere and ready to assist me with this claim, do respond to this message so i can give you the detailed information on how to proceed on this inheritance claim. Thank you.

Sincerely,

James Oliver
Attorney at law (ESQ).
jamesoliver_

■ ■ ■

FROM THE DESK OF: MR. FRANK LINARD.
DIRECTOR,INTERNATIONAL REMITTANCE
FOREIGN OPERATIONS DEPT,
UNION BANK OF NIGERIA PLC,
LAGOS-NIGERIA.

RE: YOUR INHERITANCE FUNDS OF $15.5M HAS BEEN GAZZETED TO BE RELEASED TO YOU.

ATTENTION:SIR/MADAM

THIS IS TO NOTIFY YOU THAT YOUR OVER DUE INHERITANCE FUNDS HAS BEEN GAZZETED TO BE

RELEASED, VIA KEY TELEX TRANSFER(KTT)-DIRECT WIRE TRANSFER TO YOU BY THE SENATE COMMITTEE FOR FOREIGN OVER DUE FUND TRANSFER. MEANWHILE,A WOMAN CAME TO MY OFFICE FEW DAYS AGO WITH A LETTER,CLAIMING TO BE YOUR TRUE REPRESENTATIVE.HERE ARE HER INFORMATIONS:

NAME JANET WHITE
BANK NAME: CITI BANK, NEW YORK.
ACCOUNT Number: 6503809428.

PLEASE,DO RECONFIRM TO THIS OFFICE ,AS A MATTER OF URGENCY IF THIS WOMAN IS FROM YOU SO THAT THE FEDERAL GOVERNMENT WILL NOT BEHELD RESPONSIBLE FOR PAYING INTO THE WRONG ACCOUNT NAME. THE RESERVE BANK GOVERNOR,EXECUTIVE,BOARD OF DIRECTORS AND THE SENATE COMMITTEE FOR FOREIGN OVER DUE INHERITTANCE FUND HAVE APPROVED AND ACCREDITED THIS REPUTABLE BANK WITH THE OFFICE OF THE DIRECTOR,INTERNATIONAL REMITTANCE / FOREIGN OPERATIONS,TO HANDLE AND TRANSFER ALL FOREIGN INHERITTANCE FUNDS THIS FIRST QUARTER PAYMENT OF THE YEAR.

KINDLY RECONFIRM TO US YOU THE FOLLOWING INFORMATIONS:
YOUR FULL NAME:
CONTACT ADDRESS:
DIRECT TELEPHON/CELL PHONE NUMBERS
OCCUPATION.

HOWEVER,WE SHALL PROCEED TO ISSUE ALL PAYMENTS DETAILS TO THE SAID MRS.WHITE,IF WE DO NOT HEAR FROM YOU WITHIN THE NEXT SEVEN WORKING. FROM TODAY.

CONGRATULATIONS IN ADVANCE.
BEST REGARDS,
DR. FRANK LINARD.
DIRECTOR, INTERNATIONAL REMITTANCE

■ ■ ■

CENTRAL BANK OF NIGERIA
INTERNATIONAL REMITTANCE DEPARTMENT
TINUBU SQUARE, LAGOS

DEAR SIR,
THIS IS TO INFORM YOU THAT YOUR SECOND
TRANSFER OF US$7.5 MILLION FROM THE CENTRAL BANK
OF NIGERIA IS READY FOR COLLECTION, SO YOU ARE TO
RECONFIRM THE REQUIREMENTS BELOW FOR ASSESSMENT
OF YOUR BANK DRAFT:

1) BENEFICIARY FULL NAME / YOUR COMPANY.
2) YOUR MAILING ADDRESS.
3) YOUR PHONE NUMBER TO REACH YOU AS SOON AS IT
ARRIVES.

IMMEDIATELY WE GET THIS INFORMATION FROM YOU, WE
SHALL START TO PROCESSING YOUR BANK DRAFT.

BEST REGARDS

MALLAM ISA DANKWAMBO
TELEPHONE:

■ ■ ■

Partner with me, it's urgent
From Jackson Graham
Imperial Finance House Limited
United-Kingdom

Dear Friend,
I am Mr. Jackson Graham, the Auditor General,
Imperial Finance House Limited, London United-Kingdom.
In the course of my auditing, I discovered a floating fund
in an account, which was opened in 1990 belonging to
a dead foreigner who died in 1999. Every effort made to
track any member of his family or next of kin has since
failed; hence I got in contact with you to stand as his next

of kin since you bear the same last name with him. He died leaving no heir or a will.

My intention is to transfer this sum of US$15.5Million Dollars in the aforementioned account to a safe account overseas. I am therefore proposing that you quietly partner with me and provide an account or set up a new one that will serve the purpose of receiving this fund.

For your assistance in this venture, I am ready to part with a good percentage of the entire funds.

After going through the deceased person's records and files, I discovered that:

(1) No one has operated this account since 1999
(2) He died without an heir or WILL; hence the money has been floating.
(3) No other person knows about this account and there was no known beneficiary.

If I do not remit this money urgently, it would be forfeited and subsequently converted to company's funds, which will benefit only the directors of my firm. This money can be approved to you legally as with all the necessary; documentary approvals in your name. However, you would be required to show some proof of claim, which I will provide you with and also guide you on how to make your applications.

Please reply so that I can send you detailed information on the modalities of my proposition. I completely trust you to keep this proposition absolutely confidential, if you are interested to work with me kindly forward below information:

Your First and Last Names:
Your Mobile/Cell Phone Numbers:
Your Telephone (Office and Home) Number:
Your Fax Number:
Occupation:
Your Age:
Your Nationality:

Please send the above information so I can reach you easily. I look forward to your prompt response.

Best Regards,
Mr. Jackson Graham
Auditor General
Imperial Finance House Ltd
United-Kingdom

■ ■ ■

Dear in Christ,

May the peace and blessing of the Lord be with you and your family. You Could be surprised why i picked you. But someone has to do it.

I am Mrs. Amberth Israel from FUJI, I am married to Deacon Larry Israel who is from the french speaking colony of Ivory Coast and until his death served as an Archdeacon in the St. James Archdeaconry in Ivory Coast West Africa for twelve years.

We were married for many years without a child. He died after a brief illness that lasted for only Eight days. Before his death we were both born again Christian. Since his death I decided not to re-marry or get a child outside my matrimonial home which the Bible is against.

When my late husband was alive he deposited the sum of $(11.8 Million) Eleven million Eight hundred thousand Dollars in one of the famous Bank here in Abidjan Ivory Coast. Recently, my Doctor told me that I would not last for the next Eight months due to cancer problem.

Having known my condition I decided to donate this fund to you so that you will utilize this money the way I am going to instruct herein. I want you to use this fund for orphanages, widows, Charity Services and propagating the word of God and to endeavor that the house of God is maintained.

The Bible made us to understand that "Blessed is the hand that giveth". I took this decision because I don't have any child that will inherit this money and it was the vow that i and my late husband made before God to use the fund to the Glory of God and service to humanity.

With God all things are possible. As soon as I receive your reply I shall give you the contact informations of the Bank manager for him to effect the transfer to your account.

Please get back to me as soon as possible so that i can send you the vital informations for the transfer. And i want you to assure me that you will act accordingly as I Stated herein.

Hoping to receive your reply.

Remain blessed in the Lord.
Your Sister In Christ,
Mrs. Amberth Israel.

■ ■ ■

Baghdad Iraq

Date: Sept/4th /2008

Attn:,

Since 2004, I have been working with the Iraqi ministry of oil as part of the British expatriate team helping with revamping this ministry. I am the team leader. The reason for contacting you is to seek your co-operation in the transfer of funds in-trust to you. Since the year 2005 my team and the contract award committee of the Iraq ministry of oil have awarded series of contracts in the oil industry that were executed by local companies in the gulf region. Some of the contracts are listed below:

1. The expansion of Pipeline network, crude oil and downstream products distribution and evacuation

2. Supply, install and maintain Explosion Proof Push Button Stations

3. The construction of Storage Tanks for Petroleum Products

The total value of these contracts was deliberately inflated to Forty-Five million United States Dollars (the actual value was thirty two million, five hundred thousand dollars). All the contracts have been completed and payments have been approved. The excess amount of twelve million, five hundred Unites States Dollars which belongs to my team. we propose to transfer to you in-trust for subsequent disbursement. In return, we have agreed amongst ourselves to offer you 15% of the subject amount, 5% shall be set aside for expenses. Our share shall be reserved in your country until we are able to come to your country to claim it. I cannot send the funds to my account in the UK because I am a civil servant and cannot defend the source of such large funds. If you are not a United States or Canada resident please do not bother to reply - we intend to invest in the United States or Canada and prefer to send our share there. Please note that I do not need your money as we have made adequate plans to finance this project . Your honesty is paramount in the successful completion of this project. Modalities have been worked out at the highest levels of government to ensure the speedy transfer of this fund within 10 business days.

Please understand that due to the current situation in Iraq and the anticipated chaos once the United States leaves Iraq, I am desperate to leave Iraq immediately upon completion of this project. Please indicate your interest by replying to this email.

Best Regards,

Kenneth Ferdinand

■ ■ ■

THIS IS FOR YOUR ATTENTION.

We wish to notify you again that you were listed as a beneficiary to the total sum of £10,600,000.00GBP (Ten Million Six Hundred Thousand British Pounds) in the codicil and last testament of the deceased. (Name now withheld since this is our second letter to you).

We contacted you because you bear the surname identity and therefore can present you as the beneficiary to the inheritance. We therefore reckoned that you could receive these funds as you are qualified by your name identity. All the legal papers will be processed in your acceptance. In your acceptance of this deal, we request that you kindly forward to us your letter of acceptance, your current telephone and fax numbers and a forwarding address to enable us file necessary documents at our high court probate division for the release of this sum of money. Please contact me via my email so that we can get this done immediately.

Yours faithfully,

Michael Graham
Associate Solicitor.

■ ■ ■

Okay, that's probably enough reading for one night. As you can see, the e-mails are very similar, also a bit different, but they are all designed to get you to BITE. Something for nothing—in this case a hell of a lot of something for zip—usually works to suck people in! Now, you are probably wondering how these e-mails could do you any harm; in fact you might be thinking that this is a great opportunity to get rich quick. No more grunt work, no more going to school, no more getting up in the morning, and no more work, period! You won't need any more hookups, money will never be an issue again.

Okay, chill. I know you're still going to take the hookups; it's hard to beat free when something falls off a truck in your driveway. But—and this is a big but—no offence, if you have been reading this book, if you are a normal person of average intelligence, then you already know that the probability of somebody you do not know, somebody who does not know you, sending you millions of dollars, is very, very, slim. Let me rephrase that: IT WILL NOT HAPPEN.

So what's the catch, what's up with this? Oh, did I forget something? Are you wondering how this works?

Here's the scoop. The amounts and reasons may change, but the ones I have investigated worked this way:

They will ask you to send them money to cover a few costs before they can complete the transaction.

First of all, they have to get your name registered in the country where the money is located. Cost: $2,600 US.

Next, they have to register you with a lawyer in their country. Cost $3,100 US.

Then they have to register your personal bank account with the agent in their country. Cost: $7,100 US.

They have to set up the transfer and official government documents. Cost: $15,000 US.

Now the money is just about on its way, but they have to pay some government officials before they can send it. Cost: $71,000 US.

Because this is an international transfer, they need another special permit. Cost: $11,000 US.

Just before it is sent to a bank in London for transfer to you tomorrow, there is a British surcharge. Cost: $21,000 US.

As long as you keep sending the money, they will keep coming up with another fee. At the end of the day, they have a lot of your cash, and a heck of a lot of your personal information, and in the twenty-first century, this is—everyone together now—BAD, BAD, BAD.

The next type of e-mail that you must delete, if it shows up, is something we call *Prize Pitch*. This scam is pretty simple; even I understand it. You receive an e-mail that indicates that you have won a contest or some other prize, even though you never entered that contest. Isn't life just grand? Isn't it wonderful that all over the world, they just keep drawing my name, or selecting me, even though I never bought a ticket or entered any contest? Please tell me why Lotto 6/49 never calls me, particularly when I keep buying their tickets? Doesn't this look a little bit like some type of fraudulent scheme, Sgt. Friday?

Here are some of the contests I have apparently won:

Pime Foundation
Via dell'Archetto 19-24,
00187 Roma, Italy.
http://www.pimeitm.pcn.net

Dear Beneficiary

You have been selected as one of the five (5) Beneficiary of ?825,000EURO each by Pime Foundation in line with our 50th anniversary in charity work all over the world.

For further inquiry and to process your cash grant, please contact our award secretary with the information below:

Name: Dr. Smith Hèraudi
Tel: +39-348-415

Email: pimefound01

Pime Foundation.
Yours faithfully,
Mrs. rosemary dante
Pime Foundation

∎ ∎ ∎

Notice that they do not have my name, but never mind the details: I have just won 825,000 Euros from a foundation that is into charity work! Ouch!

Here are some others:

∎ ∎ ∎

Your email address as indicated was drawn and attached to ticket number 001768432463 with serial numbers

FTS/8070337201/06 and drew the lucky numbers
15-22-24-48-50-37(30) which subsequently won you
1,000,000.00 (One Million Great Britain Pounds) from
the U.K. The draws registered as Draw number one was
conducted in Brockley, London United Kingdom on the
26th july 2008. Find below the details of the Claims Agent
and contact him with the following details for verifications:

1.FULL NAME,2.FULL ADDRESS,3.NATIONALITY,4.AGE,
5.OCCUPATION, 6.MOBILE/TELEPHONE NUMBER,7.
DATE OF WINNING AWARD, 8. SEX, 9.TOTAL AMOUNT
WON,10.TICKET NUMBERS.

NAME: Mr Mark Albert (claims agent)
E MAIL: mrmarkalbert1@

Regards
Mrs Rita Shawn

■ ■ ■

**Yes, 1,000,000 Pounds; just because they attached my
e-mail address to a ticket. You will notice that they
want a lot of personal information—the beginnings of
ID theft!**

■ ■ ■

Dear Lucky Winner,

THE HEINEKEN COMPANY SEASONAL PROMOTION

We are pleased to inform you of the result of the just
concluded annual final draws of Heineken Annual Promo.
The online Heineken Annual Promo draws was conducted
by a random selection of email addresses from an exclusive
list of 29,031 E-mail addresses of individuals and corporate
bodies picked by an advanced automated random
computer (TOPAZ) search from the internet. However, no
tickets were sold but all email addresses were assigned to
different ticket numbers for representation and privacy.

After this automated computer ballot, your e-mail address emerged as one of (12) twelve winners in the fourth category for the second prize with the following data:

Ref Number: ASL/941OYI/02/SHYNBatch Number: HGL-14/28/0046

Ticket Number: 025-11464992-750

You as well as the other winners are therefore to receive a cash prize of 250,000.00 (TWO HUNDRED AND FIFTY THOUSAND POUNDS STERLING) each from the total payout.

Your prize award has been insured with your e-mail address and will be transferred to you upon meeting the requirements, statutory obligations, verifications, validations and satisfactory report. Please note that your lucky winning number falls within our regional booklet office in your country as indicated in your play coupon.

To begin the claims processing of your prize winnings you are advised to contact our licensed and accredited Processing manager/security company for SECOND category winners with the information below: You are required to fill and SUBMIT the following information's to the Processing manager via email below.

NAME: ....
AGE: .... SEX: ....
ADDRESS: ....
PHONE: ....
OCCUPATION: ....
COMPANY:...
ANNUAL INCOME: .... NEXT OF KIN...........................
STATE..
COUNTRY: ....
NATIONALITY ....

Your Reference and Batch number at the top of this mail: Please you are advised to complete the form and send it immediately to our Processing manager through email for prompt collection of your fund.

Overseas Claims /Contact Person: Mr. Ginger Kelvin
Email: heniken.claimpromo@
Phone: +1-360-350-

S.W 20541 Washington.

NOTE: *All winnings must be claimed within 10 days
from today. After this date all unclaimed funds would be
included in the next stake.
        *Remember to quote your reference information in
all correspondence with your Processing Manager. *You
are to keep all lotto information away from the general
public especially your reference and ticket numbers.
(This is important as a case of double claims will not
be entertained). *Members of the affiliate agencies are
automatically not allowed to participate in this program.

        Note that this program was largely promoted and
sponsored by a group of philanthropist, industrialists
from the internet hardware industry and some other big
multinational firms who wish to be anonymous.

        Thank you and accept our congratulations once
again!

        Yours faithfully,

        Mr. Brown Clifton HEINEKEN Games/Lottery
        Coordinator. You must be of legal drinking.

■ ■ ■

**I know it seems unbelievable, but yes, another 250,000
Pounds. I may never have to work again!**

■ ■ ■

SOUTH AFRICAN WORLD CUP 2010 FREE LOTTERY DRAW
HEADQUARTERS. LIVERPOOL, LONDON UK.
PO BOX 1010

Dear Winner,

We are pleased to announce you as one of the 10 lucky winners in our Free Lotto Draw held by UTC/GMT is 22:18 on ,wednesday 9th of July 2008. Your email address emerged along side with the nine others as a category of winners in this year's Annual free lottery draw.

All 10 winning email addresses were randomly selected from a batch of 50,000,000 international emails. You have therefore been approved to claim a total sum of US$500,000.00 (Five Hundred Thousand United States Dollars).

In addition to your winning, you have been selected as one of they 85 lucky winners to watch the Fifa World Cup 2010 live in South Africa.

The World Cup 2010 Free Lottery Draw are proudly sponsored by these famous companies: Adidas, Coca Cola, Kia Motors, Nokia, MTN, Emirates, Toyota, Toshiba, Dell computers and mostly by the South African Government.

The South African World Cup 2010 Free Lottery Draw is held once a year. This free lottery draw is to show appreciation to global world and to encourage football soccer world wide.

We are proud to say that US$5,000,000.00 (Five Million United States Dollars) are been won annually in more than 152 countries world wide. The following particulars are attached to your lotto payment order:

    i) Winning Numbers: FL/371/-4385/6711/UK
    ii) Email Ticket Number: FL/754/22/76/UK
    iii) Lotto code Number: FL/096/22/UK
    iv) File Ref Number: FL/0473/6207/152/UK

To file your claims of US$500,000.00 (Five Hundred Thousand United States Dollars), you have to fill the below information completely and submit to our fiduciary claims agent for documentation and processing of your lottery winning certificate:

yOUR SURNAME . . . .
YOUR FIRST/MIDDLE NAMES . . . .
YOUR NATIONALITY . . . .

YOUR PRESENT ADDRESS . . . .
YOUR SEX GENDER . . . .

YOUR AGE . . . .
YOUR OCCUPATION . . . .
YOUR MOBILE PHOne number . . . .

CONTACT THE AUTHORIZED CLAIMING AGENT FOR YOUR
PRIZE.
MR MARVIN KIT WILLS

E-mail: mr.marvink@yahoo.com
Phone Number: +447024021617.

YOUR ADDRESS HAS WON

On behalf of the Board of Trustees of South African
Football Association (SAFA) Draw Promotion, kindly accept
our warmest congratulations.

Sincerely,
Rev. John Williams
Promotions Manager
FIFA World CupT Sponsors

∎ ∎ ∎

**Yeah, I know—another 500,000 US. What can I say? I'm
luckier than I ever dreamed. Who knew?**

∎ ∎ ∎

Hello,

Compliments of the day. I am Mrs. Janei Kong, The
Public Relation Officer(PRO.) of the above company. This
company is into the supply of Home Textiles, Engine Parts,

Stationery and China wares. This company was established in 2004, under the Company and Allied Matter with the Corporate Affairs Commissions of China. Having gone through a methodical search, I decided to contact you hoping that you will find this proposal interesting. we are interested in employing your services to work with us as a private payment agent.

Most of our customers pay out in cheques and money orders and we do not have an account in your country. This is the reason we are looking for a representative in your country. Also It is important to let you know that, as our representative, you will receive 10% of whatever amount you clear for the company and the balance will be for the company.

Please if you are interested to work with us in good faith And honesty, contact Dr Meng Wang, the Chief Executive Officer (CEO.) of this company through this Email address: accountdept_mengwang01@

With the following informations:
FULL NAMES . . . .
FULL ADDRESS . . . .
SEX . . . .
AGE . . . .
TELEPHONE . . . .
FAX . . . .
OCCUPATION . . . .
COMPANY NAME . . . .
COUNTRY . . . .

Endeavor to let him know that I directed you to him. Thanks for your time and remain blessed.

Very Respectfully,
Mrs. Janei Kong (PRO).

MengleiImport & Export Co. Ltd.
Goods for Import, Freight Fwdg. Svcs.

■ ■ ■

All this money, and now a job to look after their money. This is my lucky day!

■ ■ ■

UNITED NATIONS H.Q
Corporate Headquarters,
91 Station Road,
Middlesex.
United Kingdom.

Congratulations!!!

The UNITED NATIONS DEVELOPMENT PROGRAM would like to notify you that you have been chosen by the board of DEVELOPMENT BOARD as the full recipient of a cash Grant/Donation for your own personal, educational, Working and business development to receive the sum of £1,000,000.000 one million pounds.

The UNITED NATIONS DEVELOPMENT PROGRAM, established 1877 by the multi-million groups and now supported by the FBI, Economic Community for West African State (ECOWAS) and the European Union (EU). You hereby have been approved a lump sum of £1, 000, 000, 00. GBP in cash credit to file ref UNDP/HW 475/08 as one of the lucky Donor , all participant were selected through a computer balloting system drawn from Nine hundred thousand E-mail addresses all over the World as part of our international promotions prog ram which is conducted annually. No ticket were sold.

Contact your allocated claims officer on the next procedures on how to claim your prize via email and telephone

Mr. Charles Morris
Email: undpclaimsdept@
Tell: +44 704 5754

NAME(MR. MRS. MISS.): . . . .
ADDRESS: . . . .
STATE: . . . .
ZIP CODE . . . .
COUNTRY: . . . .
TEL: . . . .
FAX:. . . . .
EMAIL ADDRESS: . . . .
OCCUPATION: . . . .
ANNUAL INCOME: . . . .
MARITAL STATUS: . . . .
DATE OF BIRTH: . . . .

You are advised to contact your claims officer with your detail as indicated in this winning Notification.

Warm Regards.
Mrs Tracy Turner
Online Announcer

■ ■ ■

Gosh, more money!

■ ■ ■

University Degree

OBTAIN A PROSPEROUS FUTURE, MONEY-EARNING POWER, AND THE PRESTIGE THAT COMES WITH HAVING THE CAREER POSITION YOUNVE ALWAYS DREAMED OF. DIPLOMA FROM PRESTIGIOUS NON-ACCREDITED UNVERSITIES BASED ON YOUR PRESENT KNOWLEDGE AND PROFESSIONAL EXPERIENCE.

If you qualify, no required tests, classes, books or examinations.

Confidentiality Assured

1-213-596-24 hours a day, 7 days a week including Sundays and Holidays

from: usmanbello12@terra.es es subject: THE PRESIDENCY
THE PRESIDENCY
PRESIDENTIAL COMMITTEE ON FOREIGN PAYMENTS
FOREIGN REMITTANCE DEPARTMENT
CENTRAL BANK OF NIGERIA {CBN}
SWIFT CREDIT CARD PAYMENT
EMAIL:usmanbello_2@myway.com
PHONE:+234-80-772-42-906:

■ ■ ■

And now another degree! I must be smarter than I thought!

Please tell me that I do not have to comment further on these e-mails. You and I both know that they are not going to just up and send little old me all that dough. You're right again, they're not going to—but they will eventually inform me that to get the cash, I have to pay various fees, and, of course, taxes. Yes, there are usually a lot of fees, and as long as you keep paying, they will come up with more fees. The closer it gets to the date your cash is about to arrive, the more fees and taxes they will require you to send.

Remember to just DELETE these e-mails!

5: FISHING/PHISHING

Is it *Fishing* or is it *Phishing*? It doesn't matter—the fraudsters are definitely trying some type of trolling, or maybe they are just sitting there with the pole and bait in the water, waiting for you to click on their link. Certainly smells like fishing! Maybe I forgot to tell you that you can also use the Internet to fish—yes, there is a whole lot of fishing going on here. CAUTION, Cyber-phishing brings to your computer clear and present DANGER! Sometimes it is just a fishing telephone call, sometimes a fishing letter, but nowadays it is probably a phishing e-mail. In any event, these e-mails are set up to sort of panic you into revealing confidential information, such as your PIN, account numbers, passwords, credit and debit card numbers, etc.

Phishing equals *fooling*. Now we have all heard many fish stories, most of them fabricated; we all know that guys see things a lot bigger than they really are! We also realize that one aspect of fraud is deception, so when the bad guys moved into the high-tech arena, it started to smell phishy. Yes, their grammar is not always the best, and yes, the text contains some gobbledygook, but this type of fishing has caught a lot of people. Once they put the bait out there, add a touch of urgency, and then threaten to keep your money tied up for a long time, many people panic.

Stop right here, right now. Can the bank tie up your money because you did not answer an e-mail? It's your money, not theirs; you will always be entitled to your own cash. Again, simply DELETE.

I should mention that Phishing is also called "Brand Spoofing." Okay, don't look at me, I am just the messenger. Some cyber jockey comes up with these names; cops would call this e-scamming, or shark surfing. Either way, they have you in deep water if you reply to them. Let me explain: these e-mails are designed to look like legitimate companies, and in some cases they try to get you to click on a link that will take you to a fraudulent site or a pop-up window. Almost all of these phishing e-mails are urgent and state that if you do not act now, your account will be frozen, or you will be denied access, or some other catastrophe will happen. **Just delete!**

Let's take a look at some of these, but remember these are NOT legitimate sites; these are cyber criminals attempting to obtain your confidential information.

■ ■ ■

Safe and sound Protection with Royal Bank online

RBC Royal Bank is constantly working to increase security for all Online Banking users.
To ensure the integrity of our online payment system, we periodically review accounts.
Your account might be restricted due to numerous login attempts into your online account. Restricted accounts continue to receive payments, but they are limited in their ability to send or withdraw funds.

To lift up this restriction, you need to confirm your online banking details.
For more protection we have sent you this message for more verification and to protect your account start below,

https://www1.royalbank.com/cgi-bin/rbaccess/ rbunxcgi?protection.asp

You are required to provide all necessary information completely and correctly otherwise, due to security reasons, we may have to close your account temporarily.
Royal Bank of Canada

This web site is operated by Royal Bank of Canada
© 1996, 2002, 2003-2008
This web site is operated by Royal Bank of Canada
Privacy | Legal | Trade-marks & Copyrights | Online Banking Security

© Royal Bank of Canada 1996, 2008

■ ■ ■

Monday, 07 Jan. 2008 at 5:04:26 EST

Access was denied for one of two reasons:

a. Incorrect attempts for the payment and unusual purchase.

b. Wrong billing address with information to verify card owner.

If you remember trying to make a payment of $580.00 on the above date and time, please select "That was me."

If you do not remember trying to make a payment of $580.00 on the above date and time, please select "That was NOT me."

This is new security system between Mastercard International and Canadian Tire MasterCard to protect you against any fraudulent internet use of your account number if the number is used without your knowledge.

© Information on this website is provided by Canadian Tire Bank, issuer of the Canadian Tire MasterCard Cards.

Please update your phone number now. We would like to be able to contact you because we detect fraudulent transactions on your account due to unauthorized activity occur without your consent in Online Banking.

Click Here to UPDATE YOUR PHONE NUMBER NOW

■ ■ ■

TD Canada Trust Online Banking Security Department.

2008 TD Group Financial

Dear Subscribers

This is To enable us complete our upgrading and maintenance on our services.

You are advice to reply to this email immediately and enter your password here [...] Failure to do this may lead to your email account deactivated from our database.

∎ ∎ ∎

Dear RBC Financial Group Customer,

Recent email scams have attempted to consume customers into disclosing their Online Banking security log-in details.

We publish details about such scams on our security pages. However, we would like to get security warnings across to customers as many as possible. That's why we're asking you to take a few minutes to check and update your account details. This will allow us to update you occasional security and Online Banking service information.

Due to the recent security update, you are requested to follow the link below.

https://www1.royalbank.com/english/netaction/sgne.html

Important

We have asked few additional information which is going to be the part of secure login process. These additional information will be asked during your future login security so, please provide all these info completely and correctly otherwise due to security reasons we may have to close your account temporarily.

RBC Financial Group
Security Advisor
RBC Financial Group.

This web site is operated by Royal Bank of Canada

Privacy | Legal | Trade-marks & Copyrights | Online Banking Security

© Royal Bank

■ ■ ■

This is to notify you that we are presently working on our Sympatico Email, this maintenance can close your Sympatico email account completely. Please do not say you were not informed, your urgent response is highly needed, to protect your email account from being closed, please forward your Username and Password to our customer services with email address: webmailupdate@yahoo.ca

****

Attention E-Mail Account Holder,

LAST NOTICE

We are currently performing maintenance for our Digital mail Account owners due to the rate of internet passwords and other information problems. And we discovered that our mail account owners have been receiving phishing mails form imposters asking for their personal informations. So we intend upgrading our Digital mail Security Server for better online services.

In order to ensure you do not experience service interruption, Please you must reply to this email immediately and enter your USERNAME here: (************) and PASSWORD here: (************) for security reasons and Check out your new features and enhancements with your new and improved mail account. To enable us upgrade your Account; for better online services please reply to this mail.

NB: We request your username and password for Identification purpose only.

■ ■ ■

Dear TD Canada Trust & TD Commercial Banking customer,

TD Group Customer Service would like to inform you that we are currently carrying out a scheduled upgrade of TD Security software.

In order to guarantee high level of security to our customers, we require you to complete "EasyWeb Form" (for TD Canada Trust customers) or "Web Business Banking Form" (for TD Commercial Banking customers).

Please select and complete your form using the link below:

http://customerform.td.com/service/serverid/form.aspx?user=5567726556697189439403269490274333039499671724789581388&id=82608936303

Thank you for being a valued customer.

Sincerely,
TD Group Customer Service

■ ■ ■

Okay—what do you think: is the bank going to close your account, take all your money, block your access, temporarily put you in the corner, etc.? No. No bank will ever threaten you or take and hold your money.

TIP #6: Financial institutions will never ask you for this type of personal information. They already have it. Just delete these e-mails. Never act on them. They are fraudulent!

If you really want to talk to somebody at your financial institution, call the telephone number on the back of your credit card or on your bank statement. NEVER use the telephone numbers or links that appear on these e-mails.

6: THE INTERNET PLUS LOVE: SOCIAL SITES, DATING SITES, AND OTHER PECCADILLOS

I think Celine sang, "Have you ever been in love?" Hey, hey, watch who's reading with you before you answer (better still, avoid the question). On the other hand, if you are looking, love is absolutely front and centre on the 'net. Talk about social or dating frenzy, it's all right here at your fingertips. No need for those blind dates that your friends set up to try and finally get their weird brothers married off! No more speed dating where you get thirty-five **no's** in one hour. And—dare I say it—no more diets or working out to try and look better; who needs all that when you've got the Internet! Millions of people all over the world, just looking for **you.** Oh! I almost forgot, no more singles dances where you keep bumping into your former marriage counsellor.

Now you can fall in love without ever leaving the house. And yes, you can be whoever you want to be: if you're short, you can be six feet tall; if you're overweight, you can be slim; if you look like you played goal without a mask, you can be a hunk; or a hottie . . . what's not to love about this? I mean you can be a doctor or a lawyer or a dentist—well, okay, nobody wants to admit to being a dentist! But come on, to get hooked up, I need only to be able to type (grammar and spelling would be good). This is great! I can use a different name and **chat** with my former significant other. Talk about a bottomless pit, or endless possibilities, there really is no limit.

So what's the problem? There is an immense problem! Who the heck are you actually chatting with? Yes, their photo is on their profile, but is that really him or her? You're chatting to some-body who from the photo appears to be an eighteen-year-old male; but is this really a male, and is he actually eighteen years old, or is he maybe fifty-five? Does the person you're chatting with have a criminal record, does he or she have convictions for sexual offences, including sexual assault or stalking? Chat rooms are totally random; in many ways it is a fantasy world, **so use extreme caution. Other than your friends, you do not know with whom, or what, you are interacting.**

A gal telephoned me a few months ago, and indicated that she had been spending some time in various chat rooms, and after chatting for thirty or forty minutes, she would realize it was her former boyfriend with whom she was chatting. Even when she left and went to another chat room, the same thing would happen. Turns out she lived in a complex that provided wireless Internet to all of the tenants, and somebody was intercepting her Internet activity. She did mention to me that her former boyfriend was a big-league computer techie. That's a double ouch—how do you get rid of him?

Last week I had a female call me. She wanted to check out a potential boyfriend whom she had met on-line, and had been out for coffee with on three evenings. She said that although he had money, he did not drive. Now a guy without a driver's licence is just not normal! There are three main reasons he would be without a licence: he has been convicted of impaired driving; he has unpaid fines; or the province has taken his licence for not paying child support. Either way, this is probably not a good candidate for a relationship. I should also mention that I found out he had a history of violence!

Social Sites sort of started as a way to communicate with friends and family. They save hundreds of e-mails and let you share photos and personal updates without making numerous telephone calls. But some of these sites will let anyone download your photo, and a lot of people place on these sites enormous amounts of information, including age, school or former school, occupation, town or city they live in, where they are going next weekend, employer, etc.

We already know that half of our criminals live on the Internet, and we certainly know that half of our sickos have joined them. If everybody were honest, reliable, and of good character, this would not be a problem. But reality is a lot different; hundreds, if not thousands, of bad people spend a lot of their time trying to use your personal information to their advantage, and many try to definitively find you.

A year ago, some reporters posed on-line as a thirteen-year-old girl, and they chatted with a number of men who eventually showed up at an address the reporters had given to spend the evening with this hypothetical, underage girl. These men came from all age groups, married and single, unemployed or working, and one guy even took a 200-kilometre bus ride to the house.

When I worked in the RCMP Security Service, many of the foreign and national spies utilized tombstone data to build a new identity, which allowed them to move around Canada without causing suspicion. Now they can go on-line and get this information, and a whole lot more. In today's world, identity theft and fraud are a fact of life, and the more you put details of your life out there, the more likely it is that somebody will eventually become you.

How does all of this work? Funny you should ask that! Very simply: I can download almost any profile or head shot from the Internet, and then download that photo onto any driver's licence or other photo identification, and now I am you. Yes, I have to find somebody who looks similar to the person who is going to use the fictitious identification, but we are talking about millions of profile photos, so it's not that difficult. You already know that with your identification, I can do anything you can do, and maybe more. Anybody that has worked as a bouncer (sorry—door safety officer) knows that a number of sixteen-to-eighteen-year-olds have actual, genuine, altered driver's licences showing that they are twenty years old.

I was talking to an RCMP member the other day who mentioned that a friend of his was trying to sell an item on-line. The individual did not get the price he was looking for, and withdrew the item. A week later, he noticed somebody selling his exact item; they had simply downloaded the photo of his item and were now selling it themselves!

Hey, I know that a good chunk of life must be *fun*, and you will be *happier and healthier* if you have as many fun times as are humanly possible. Make life happen, enjoy, live a little, or a lot, but try to limit the amount of information about yourself and your family that can be viewed and utilized by all of the bad guys in the world.

This is important! TIP #7 When you hook up to the Internet, you must protect your computer and your information.

Most Internet providers will also offer some type of protection or security package. Do the work, do the research, and make sure you purchase the following:

Anti-virus software; prevents viruses from infecting your computer

A firewall; keeps out hackers and unwanted connections

Anti-spyware software; stops hackers from stealing your confidential information

In addition,

• **Change your user name and password regularly**.

• **Back up your important files.**

So we are now at the end of the chapters on the Internet, but before I move on, we have to talk again, and not just a good old family around the dinner table type of talk, although I hope you are holding these very frequently. Now, this is one of those good-guy cop one-on-ones that I hope will keep you out of one of the oldest Internet scams that I can think of. Yes, even as we speak, somebody, somewhere, is getting the crap kicked out of his pocketbook because he just got sucked into it!

Now, maybe I should put this one in my next book; but hey, if you bought this book, and one for your aunt Winnie in

Gravelburg, and of course your family in Bigger (hopefully three for the family in Bigger), then don't panic. I will not scam you—I am the one guy you can trust. Yeah, I know—every time I say this, I get, "Terry, I never trust anyone who says 'trust me'!" But you know what? It's pretty good advice, particularly if the person who said it is trying to sell you something.

Get ready—here it is. Think about how many times you have read or heard about this in the past few years.

This scam starts off with your selling something on the Internet; let's say you are trying to get $1,299 for the item. Eventually a buyer comes along and purchases the item for $1,299, BUT—and yes, this is a very big but—sends you $2,200 instead of the $1,299. Great—or is it? Step back for a minute and look at the big picture. When is the last time anyone sent you $900 more than you were asking? **Memo to self:** it does not happen; it never happens. If you or I are not sure of the asking price, even though it is sitting right there on the computer screen, we are going to contact the seller to confirm the price before we send payment. I might send you an extra ten or twenty dollars if I am not sure of the price (okay, I am a cop, maybe an extra two dollars), but under no circumstances will I send you an extra $900. **Yikes! This has to be a tipoff that something is amiss. If you have read the book up to this point, then you already know that this is a huge problem!**

So what happens next? Now comes the sting: you are sitting there with a cheque, or a bank draft, or a money order, or a postal money order, etc, for $2,200 (maybe I should mention that all of the above methods of payment are counterfeit, stolen, or altered). Now the purchaser contacts you, just when you thought you had made a killing. The scenario goes something like this:

Hi, I just realized that I made a mistake/ it appears my secretary sent you too much money in error/ somehow we sent you $900 more than you wanted/ how much was that money order I sent you?/ I bought two items over the Internet and sent the wrong cheque to you . . .

Take your choice of the above.

Now here comes the **carrot.** Bad guy says, Look, you have gone to some bother here, I have caused you to do some stuff on your own time, so let's do this—for all of your trouble, keep a hundred dollars, and send me back $801.

These bad guys are just too kind! If you follow through and try to deposit the $2,200 (yes, I know—from reading this book, you knew right off the bat that this smelled a heck of a lot like fraud, but you decided to put it to the test), your bank manager will have some bad news for you. But as to your great Uncle Gilles in Conception Bay South, for whom you forgot to buy this book, he's about to get a $2,200 debit posted to his bank account.

> **TIP#8 No matter what method of payment you receive, do not do anything with your item until the payment instrument has been cleared by your financial institution, even if it takes weeks to clear.**

> **TIP#9 If you are selling items on-line, take a look at, and do some research on, something called PayPal.**

This sort of reminds me of an investigation I worked on, where the perpetrator, a thirty-five-year-old woman who was the manager of a group of thirty-five individuals, started buying dinner for the group a few times a month, and paid for the meals and drinks personally. Now I don't know about you, but yes, I would like to work there a few evenings a month. On the other hand, this is not normal and should have raised a red flag, or several red flags. Even the chief executive officer was not *that* rich! Where did she get all of her money? Yes, you guessed it: over a million dollars from the company till. One of the first signs that you might be about to deal with fraud is that fraud is usually too good to be true.

Just before I finish this chapter, I have to tell you about another Internet scam that is becoming very popular. Now keep in mind that these things work because there is no face-to-face interaction, and remember, this makes fraudsters a lot bolder. I expect that, having read the book up to this point, *you* could think of a number of schemes or scams that the bad guys could use.

This one involves those individuals who advertise rental properties over the Internet. The criminals see your ad and contact you and indicate that their daughter is starting university and needs an apartment; or their mother is moving to the area and this is a great location for her; or their grandmother needs a place close to a medical facility; and so on. A couple of days later, you receive the first and last month's rent and ten postdated cheques. No problem, right? Well, there may not be a problem, unless they contact you prior to the moving-in date to say that daughter is not going to university, or mother is not going to move, etc. You are then directed to refund the money. You guessed it, the cheques they gave to you were all fraudulent, and the bank will eventually debit your account for the amount of the cheques that you deposited, because they were fraudulent items. As per Tip # 8, **make no refunds until their method of payment has cleared your account.**

I just took a break from writing and checked my e-mail; look what I found there:

■ ■ ■

Zürich Lotterien
Central Office.
Management and Central Services:
Weg 205 B - 02241, zum Erfolgreichen, Switzerland.

From The Promotions Department of Zürich Lotterien.

We are pleased to inform you of the result of the just concluded annual final draws of Zürich Lotterien Program.

After this automated computer ballot, your e-mail address attached to serial number 02-87-87 drew the lucky numbers 4-11-41-26-02-62, which consequently emerged you as one of first ten (10) lucky winners in the United Kingdom category.

You have therefore been approved for a lump sum pay off of €1,000,000.00 (One Million EURO) in cash credited to file ZL/08/4008. This is from total cash prize of €50 Million Euro shared amongst the first fifty- (50) lucky winners all around the world. Your funds are now deposited in an offshore bank with a hardcover insurance.

Please note that your lucky winning number falls within our European booklet representative office in London. In view of this, our affiliate bank in the Europe would release your €1,000,000.00 (One Million Euro) to you in the United Kingdom.

To claim your prize funds, you are required to come directly to our UK office for direct claim. If you have problems with coming to our office you can make a wire transfer of your funds to your private bank account. You can also employ the use of a courier service company to deliver your winning cheque to your home or office address.

For a telegraphic transfer of your funds to your private bank account, you are required to send your name and address in full, phone number, bank name, bank address, next of kin, account number, Swift/Routing/Sort Code, so as to facilitate the release of your funds to your stated bank account.

For a courier service delivery, you are required to send your name, phone number, information of next of kin, mailing address (home or office address), so as to facilitate the release of your Funds to your desired address.

You are required to send the necessary information as regards your chosen option to our help line below:

Zürich Lotterien
Information and Payment Bureau:
London Representative Office
Help | Service | Contact

E-mail: zurichloto@g

You will be assisted in the processing and remittance of your prize funds as regards your chosen option.

Congratulations once again from all members and staff and thanks for being part of our promotions program.

Knute Fredriech
Public Relations,
Zürich Lotterien

∎ ∎ ∎

What am I going to do with this? Just delete, thank you!

7: DEFENCES

Somebody once said that the best defence is a good offence.
When it comes to fraud, a good defence is some defence.

THE POST OFFICE; MAIL

Let's talk a little bit about your mail—something that we take for granted, give little thought to, unless it starts to disappear. At first, it's just dinner table conversation: "Any mail today?" Somebody says no, didn't see any. Who cares—it will come tomorrow, or if not, then the next day. No big deal, right?

Wrong! If I can read your mail, I can find out a lot about your life; if I can read it over a period of time, I know your life. Your mail is a critical item in the fight against identity theft. Many thieves take the position that everybody works, and that after 8:30 a.m. nobody is at home. Now, they watch for the mail person (yes, many places in Canada still have home mail delivery), wait a few minutes until he/she has walked on, and then will either take your mail right then, or, if they are somewhat sophisticated criminals, they will ring your doorbell first to make sure you are not at home. Think about how much information someone can acquire by stealing your mail. For example, bank statements, credit card statements, life insurance policies, government documentation and cheques, those items wrapped in plain brown paper, etc. This stuff contains a windfall in biographical information, and they had to work only a few minutes to get it!

And yes, there are in fact thefts from the Canada Post Corner Super boxes. Whether you have a Corner Super Box or a residential mailbox, try to pick up the mail as soon after delivery as possible and never leave mail in the box overnight.

TIP #10: Purchase a residential mailbox that can be locked.

REDIRECTING YOUR MAIL

Criminals always seem to find the easy way to do things. Why should they take a chance of getting caught stealing your mail? Why not just have your mail sent directly to them!

This is one of the oldest schemes perpetrated against individuals: the redirecting of their mail. Someone with identification in your name simply goes to the post office and changes your address. The address is normally changed to that of a mail drop (a mail drop is any organization that provides mail boxes), e.g., Shoppers Drug Mart, Mail Boxes, etc., or the post office. Remember, when bad guys rent a post office box, they disguise it by using the word *suite*.

No more bills, no more flyers, no more summons . . . this is great! Wait a second, stop celebrating! This is actually a problem. If you notice the volume of your daily mail has been diminishing or has stopped altogether, contact Canada Post Customer Service at the following number to insure that your mail has not been redirected: 1–800–267–1177.

If you are going to be away from home for any period of time, it is recommended that you have someone you trust remove your mail on a daily basis, or contact Canada Post and utilize their *Hold Mail* service.

Go to your local post office or on-line at **www.canada-post.ca** and file a Hold Mail Request.

Remember to shred all mail that includes any biographical information on you or other family members before disposing of it. For example, many corporations and charities send unsolicited promotional materials that include your full name and address; these should be shredded. And don't forget to always empty your residential mail box daily.

It should be noted that in today's world it is paramount that when you change your permanent address, none of your mail goes back to your former address. If you have ever gone to a condo or apartment building mail room, there is sometimes mail all over the place; make sure none of it is yours. Utilize the services of Canada Post, and ensure that you have notified all financial institutions and credit issuers with your new address.

A couple of years ago, we were conducting surveillance on a gang that we believed were stealing mail. They were utilizing the "slow walker" manoeuvre. This is where an individual follows the mail delivery person early in the morning, particularly if mail is being delivered to business premises, prior to opening. Once the mail delivery person turns the corner, the "slow walker" collects the delivered mail. The "slow walker" is basically looking for corporate cheques. The cheques are then altered, washed, and razed and utilized by the criminals to make payments. They might even send one to you, to rent your apartment or to purchase items that you are selling on the Internet.

> **Tip #11: Please ensure that when you move, all of your mail is sent to your new address, and think about using the Hold Mail service for thirty days after you have moved. Also be sure to purchase a residential mailbox that locks.**

GARBAGE

We have reached that point in the book where we have to talk about a very unpleasant subject. Relax, I know it's disgusting, but I have to talk about it. Yes, the subject stinks, and yes, nobody ever wants to just pick this topic up and run with it; in fact, you usually had to be asked a number of times by good old Mom before you would ever take it outside.

When you think about how simple it is to perpetrate identity theft, surely there cannot be anything simpler than picking through someone's garbage. Just imagine losing thousands of dollars out of your bank account because your own personal garbage did you in! Please tell me what could be simpler for a fraudster than taking some of the garbage that you are trying to get rid of anyway and utilizing it for unlawful purposes? Does it make any sense for you to lock everything up, buy different types of insurance, regularly check your account statements, and then just throw it all in the garbage?

One of the simplest ways of acquiring information on anyone is to take her garbage. In today's world, most of us segregate paper waste, such as documents, from other garbage, placing the documents in the blue box and the garbage in bags. Bad guys who usually do a lot of their work at night anyway, look through your blue box contents once you place it at the curb. Unfortunately, when I had to sift though garbage, they did not have blue boxes, so we had to open up and look through the actual garbage and separate the paper waste ourselves from sardines, macaroni, and fish sticks. We usually did this in July, naturally, but also we usually had a junior man present to do the heavy sorting!

Where possible, place your garbage at the curb the morning of pickup, and shred all documents containing personal information.

Where trash is placed in dumpsters, or containers outside of your home or business, identity theft perpetrators also check these areas (dumpster diving).

SHRED EVERYTHING!

Today we are constantly receiving unsolicited materials that in some cases contain our full names and addresses. Some of these materials may be applications for credit cards; other items may be from the federal government and may include your SIN. **Never** throw these items into your garbage or recycle bins. They must be shredded. Any items or materials that you place in the garbage that contain any biographical information about you or other members of your family leaves you extremely vulnerable to identity fraud. Never let your garbage be the one item that actually exposes you. **Shred**.

From the lowest-level street gangs to the very sophisticated, high-end gangs, and everyone else in between, it's simple to perpetrate identity fraud, the rewards are significant, and the chances of being caught are minimal. At the very end of the day, all they really need is your non-shredded garbage.

TIP#12: **Buy a shredder and set up a recycle basket in the house. Shred all sensitive materials before you place them at the curb.**

THE NEXT TIER OF DEFENCE

Now that we have established our first line of defence, and have decided to control our garbage and mail, making them a hard target, this will normally force bad guys onto the soft targets. At the same time, cutting off two of the ways that criminals can acquire our biographical information makes our identities a lot safer. Most people, criminals included, will usually take the easier route to their eventual goal: the criminals will simply move on to the unlocked mailbox, or the non-shredded contents of the blue box. So now we have to move on up to the next defensive tier and sort of set up what the police would term our "intelligence-gathering phase."

Don't fret, this is not sophisticated, is not time-consuming, every one of you will understand it, and that's why we have to do it. This intelligence phase will immediately identify attacks on most of your financial assets. It will give you the ability to detect the financial institution or product that they are attempting to defraud and put the criminals out of business before they get into full swing.

This phase is kind of humorous, because basically the one and only thing that will allow you to avoid becoming a target of identity theft is a *poor financial profile*. Yes, if yours is below the sub-basement, or if it's so bad that you can't get a monthly transit pass without a co-signer, criminals will probably never attack what is left of your not-so-good name!

R-9, the lowest credit rating, the one that identifies those slow to pay or who never pay, or are bankrupt—that will keep the bad guys away; but at the same time you're going to have a pretty Spartan lifestyle!

So, second tier, cornerstone of our intelligence program, is . . . come on, what do you think it is? What is the one thing that could do all of the things I have mentioned above? Okay, everybody that said, "Your personal credit profile!" stand up and give yourself a pat on the back. Hey, you may even be in line for a promotion!

CREDIT BUREAUS

The credit bureau can both surface the fact that you have been targeted, and at the same time offer you invaluable assistance if you are a victim of ID fraud.

The credit bureau is like a national collection house that retains records of your credit history and present credit standing. For example, any time you attempt to acquire financing (loans, lines of credit, or mortgages), credit cards, cellular telephones, automobiles, or any item that you are purchasing through monthly payments, the corporation supplying the goods or services checks your credit history at a credit bureau prior to advancing funds or closing the deal.

With regard to the above, if someone attempts to acquire almost anything in your name (through identity theft), the place where they are attempting to acquire goods, services, or financing will make an inquiry at a credit bureau prior to completing the transaction. This inquiry will show up on your credit history. **As a result, you can tell, by means of the Credit Bureau, if someone has taken over your identity** by simply obtaining your credit history and checking the inquiries section. If there are inquiries from any financial institution or other type of company that you have not been dealing with, somebody is probably using your identification to acquire something. Notify the credit bureau immediately.

It should be noted that in Canada there are two credit bureaus, and they are competitors; as a result, you probably need to check both.

1. TRANSUNION

You have two options for requesting a copy of your TransUnion Consumer Disclosure:

Option One: Make immediate on-line access for a fee of $14.99 (applicable taxes are included). This service will provide you with a copy of your credit report and a credit bureau score.

Option Two: Mail your request to the Consumer Relations Department and receive your file, free of charge, via Canada Post.

> **TransUnion of Canada**
> P.O. Box 338 LCD 1
> Hamilton, Ontario
> L8L 7W2
> Tel: 1–800–663–9980
> Tel: 1–877–713–3393 (for Quebec)

2. EQUIFAX

You have two options for requesting a copy of your Equifax Consumer Disclosure:

Option One: Make immediate access via on-line service for a fee of $15.50 (applicable taxes are included). This service will provide you with a copy of your credit report and a credit bureau score.

Option Two: Mail your request to the Consumer Relations Department and receive your file, free of charge, via Canada Post.

> **National Consumer Relations**
> P.O. Box 190, Station Jean-Talon
> Montreal, Quebec
> H1S 2Z2
> Tel: 1–800–465–7166
> Fax: (514) 355–8502
> E-mail: **consumer.relations@equifax.com**

3. EXPERIAN
1–888–397–3742

It should be noted that some of the credit bureaus allow you to obtain your credit via the telephone.

If you are a victim of fraud: Contact TransUnion's and Equifax's Fraud Victim Assistance Departments to place fraud alerts on your credit files.

TransUnion
Fraud Victim Assistance Department
P.O. Box 338, LCD 1
Hamilton, Ontario
L8L 7W2

Equifax Credit Information Services
Consumer Fraud Division
Box 190 Jean Talon Station
Montreal, Quebec
H1S 2Z2

Okay, is everybody ready? Let's set up your entire defensive align-
ment. But just before we do that, I want to add a few more parts.
I want your defence to resemble the old Chicago Bears D, and
just like when you had to play in Soldiers Field in Chicago, you
might make some short gains here and there, but you're going
to be black and blue after! The following seven components are
your defensive safety net. If you keep them working for you on
an ongoing basis, you will be able to detect almost anyone who
attempts to tamper with your finances.

INTERNET BANKING

So, right off the bat we are going to rely heavily on Internet
banking to alert us if somebody is trying to pull an end run on
any of our accounts, or trying to utilize any of our credit or debit
cards, or has a counterfeit version of any of our cards.

Just a little refresher: When you get set up for Internet
banking, this allows you to examine on a daily basis all of your
credit union or bank accounts and all of your credit card accounts.
You can see all of the credits, debits, and purchases, including
debit and point-of-sale activity daily. Stop waiting until you get
your monthly statements—you are giving these criminals an
extra thirty days to keep taking your money—just check your
accounts on-line and cut these people off when they first start
to attack. Let's not help them take your dough. Get these creeps
stopped right now!

PERSONAL CREDIT REPORT

Be sure to check the inquiries section and make sure that no one is trying to put you in the red zone by acquiring credit in your good name. If there are inquiries from companies that you have never dealt with, or do not recognize, notify the credit bureau immediately and buy into some of their fraud or identity theft programs. Also, remember that some financial institutions offer free fraud programs and credit checks.

YOUR RESIDENTIAL OR BUSINESS GARBAGE

Before you toss that stuff to the outside, let's shred everything. Remember, the criminals would love to do you in through your own mistakes. Stop assisting them; shred your documents before they are placed in the garbage or recycle box. YES, SHRED!

YOUR MAIL

Be sure to take all of the precautions necessary to ensure that your mail is not delivered to your former place of residence. At the same time, ensure that your mail has not been redirected. Now we all know that an integral part of any defence is interceptions; however, you must make sure that no one is intercepting your mail once it is delivered. Lock it down, get that box that locks, and keep the thieves away from your delivered mail.

YOUR RESIDENTIAL TITLE

Periodically ensure that your residential title has not been switched. Also think about purchasing Title Insurance. Although we have a very good defence, insurance acts to nullify those little weaknesses that may pop up due to human error. As my kids keep reminding me, we all make mistakes!

E-MAIL SCAMS

NEVER act on the e-mail scams we have already examined in this book—just delete them. The same goes for telephone messages that indicate you have won something: just delete; ignore them. NEVER give out credit card information to any of the above! I need not remind you about the impossibility of getting something for nothing, but remember that is exactly what this is. DELETE!

LOCKING AND SECURING

All identification not on your person must be secured; do not leave it lying around the house. Dramatically limit the number of credit cards, and debit cards, and the amount of identification that you carry on your person.

POST-GAME RECAP

We all dislike those Monday morning quarterbacks, but remember, if you stay with our defence regime, you are going to expeditiously recognize attacks on your assets by limiting the amount of personal financial and biographical information available in the public domain. These defensive postures are not time-consuming. A couple of them are lifestyle, and a couple mean five minutes a day at your computer. Do not procrastinate; you can do this. It's really quite simple. No excuses: JUST DO IT! (And yes, use your **delete** button extremely liberally.)

Cops love to say, "Oh, sorry, Inspector, I don't think I got that memo!" Hey, no excuses from you guys! Keep yourself and your family safe. Buy into my defence protocol and keep all of your money working for *you*, not the criminals. Don't live dangerously. Why take a chance? This involves only a few minutes of your time on a fairly regular basis.

I am reminded of the time I was serving subpoenas on the Six Nations at Oshwegan, Ontario. I pulled into a long driveway, got out of the car, and walked up to the side door of the house. I knocked on the door, but no one appeared to be around. At this point, I noticed a large sign on the door that read something like this: "Property protected by shotgun security, three days a week." You guess which days. As I stepped back, I observed five deer hanging from a large tree in the back of the house. Thank God my training kicked in! I hastily retreated to the car, deciding to go back to the office and give this subpoena to a junior man to serve!

8: OFFENCES

Here's just a little more reinforcement on how huge a problem identity theft is in Canada. You might recall that in October 2007 the then Federal Justice Minister Rob Nicholson mentioned that the government intended to get tough on criminals involved in identity theft. Here is a brief look at some of the headlines that flowed from that statement:

IDENTITY THEFT RAPIDLY GROWING THANKS TO TECHNOLOGY.

CANADIAN COUNCIL OF BETTER BUSINESS ESTIMATES IDENTITY THEFT COSTS CONSUMERS, BUSINESSES, AND THE FINANCIAL SECTOR NEARLY $2 BILLION EACH YEAR.

CANADIAN BANKERS' ASSOCIATION CALLS THE GOVERNMENT'S COMMITMENT A MUCH-NEEDED STEP FORWARD.

Houston, I think we have a problem. If you have been reading the newspaper for the past few years, you already know there is a huge problem; if we were just a bit skeptical before, we now all realize that if the government is going to step in, the problem must be nearly totally out of control!

CREDIT CARDS

Don't even say the word out loud if you are in a public place! Nothing in this world attracts criminals as expeditiously as a credit card. Bad guys have literally hammered the crap out of credit cards for a number of years, and getting their hands on your credit card is something they spend a lot of their time working on. Just like bees to honey, cops and criminals to strip clubs, guys to girls (or is that girls to guys?), Jamaicans to ackee and salt fish, nothing attracts or makes crooks salivate like your good old credit cards. I mean, think about it—for crooks, it's money in the bank. What else, what other instrument, has so many different types of fraudulent schemes attached to it? Okay, your debit card, good point, but that's it. Seems like everything they have tried has worked; I almost need a separate book to list all of the various and sundry ways criminals can obtain and utilize your credit card!

I suppose you're wondering if the crooks are looking for a needle in a haystack or for green jelly beans. (I only mention the green jelly beans because at the conclusion of a three-week RCMP course, one of the corporals mentioned that on the way home he was going to stop and buy five or six pounds of green jelly beans. When I asked why, he said that he was going to toss them around the back yard grass for the kids to find while he spent a bit of uninterrupted time with his wife.)

Okay, where was I . . . oh, yes, is it difficult for criminals to find credit cards? Let's put it this way: there are over sixty million credit cards in circulation across Canada; you can figure out how many are being used every second of the day. Please don't ask me, I took the *old* math, but yes, it's tons. Like you, I'm also wondering what percentage of credit card transactions is fraudulent. Now, from what I have heard, annual sales volumes are over $200 billion, and at this point in time, payment card fraud is in the neighbourhood of $300 million. With this type of feast out there, you can see why criminals have more than a passing interest in credit cards.

I don't want to dwell on this much longer, but crooks and credit cards almost go hand in hand (that is, your credit card and their hand). I feel your pain, but why don't we get their hands back where they belong—in handcuffs! Credit card fraud is not impossible to stop. If we can just do a little bit of work together, we can dramatically reduce the millions of dollars lost to credit card fraud. I will even give you guys your gold shield back, maybe! Yes, make you honorary detectives, but you have to promise me that you well follow my detection strategy, and then in the same breath, notify the card issuer. I mean, does it get any better? Just a bit of good old fun detective work, for a few seconds every day, and HELLO, we can make the criminals cringe! Yes, we can bruise the bad guys, and yes, we can outfox those fools.

Ways They Can Obtain Your Card

There are a lot of categories here, and you already know that you can't detect or stop fraudulent methods that you are not aware of or that you do not understand, so explanations galore are coming right up; but just before we get started, here's a tip:

> **TIP#13: Make a list of all of your credit cards and the telephone numbers that appear on the back of the cards. Secure this information—yes, lock this list up.**

Never, ever, let your credit card out of your sight. Do not get sidetracked when you hand it to anyone for payment, and, just in case, look at the card when it is handed back to be sure it's your card. Please don't get fooled!

Ready, here we go!

Lost

The last thing I hope I lose is my credit card, but as soon as I get to McDonalds or Tim's for supper, I will know it's gone! Hopefully any time you lose your card, you will also know it's gone by the end of the day. The problem we have here is that if I find your card I can shop with it. When is the last time any merchant ever checked your signature or asked for other ID? It never happens, right?

I have often thought that a credit card should contain age and sex, because if you have a name like mine, Terry, a man or woman could use it. But it may be a moot point anyway, because very few merchants ever look at the name. I was speaking in the U.S. last year, and when I was introduced, I entered from the back of the room. As I walked past the first couple of rows, I heard one of the men say, "Holy ****—it's a guy!" Did I mention that my first name is Leslie?

If you have lost your card, notify your credit card issuer immediately. Even if you do not have the card number, they can still probably find you by name. But let them know right away. Some issuers will even place a temporary freeze on your card, in case you find it within a short time.

Some time back, we were conducting surveillance on an individual that we believed had stolen credit cards in his possession. At approximately eleven a.m. on a Tuesday morning in July, he entered a bank in downtown Toronto and attempted to obtain a $5,000 cash advance on a credit card. The teller gave him a voucher to sign, and then compared the signature on the voucher to the signature on the credit card. She then asked the chap to sign another voucher, stating that the two signatures were not even close. Do you want to know the rest of the story? I hate to tell you this: the teller still was not happy, and so she asked Mr. Bad Guy to sign yet another voucher! This time she was cool, and gave our bad guy the $5,000, and now unfortunately you know the rest of the story.

STOLEN

This category relates to cards stolen from the cardholder. You must treat credit cards the same way criminals do: like they are cash. Crooks can use your card themselves, or they can sell it to another criminal. So where are cards likely to be stolen? Well, a great place to steal cards is at your workplace, because most people trust their co-workers. Now this is a good thing, but do not tempt anyone. If you are leaving your workstation, take your purse or wallet with you. Better still, lock them up, or keep them close to or on your person, but never in plain view!

When you start looking at all of the empirical studies of crime in the workplace that have been conducted at several US universities, it becomes clear that people base their criminal intent on the risk of getting caught. Minor- or no-risk crime happens! These studies also indicate that if you put a hundred people in a room, ten percent of them will spend a lot of their day thinking about ways to rip off the company or their co-workers.

A lot of cards are stolen at places where people have lockers: the gym, health club, golf club, swimming pool, etc. Believe me, it is best not to leave anything of value in an unattended locker.

Be extremely leery about anyone at your club with bolt cutters in his or her golf bag!

A few years ago, I commenced an investigation for a financial institution that had hired a university student for the summer. The student had worked as a teller, which means that she had her own cash drawer that was locked up in her own teller's locker when not in use. The teller was the only person who had the combination to her teller's locker. Her teller's cash drawer contained between five to eight thousand dollars in cash. A couple of weeks before summer ended, it was announced that the student had been hired as a part-time teller and would be working every other weekend. Our student left at the end of summer, returned two weeks later, removed her cash drawer from her locker, and discovered that all of her cash had been removed. This is what we call a mysterious disappearance of cash. Remember, give bad guys something of value, locked in an unattended locker, and then give them some time to work out a plan, and you're apt to have a problem!

If your card has been stolen, notify the credit card issuer immediately.

Not Received

Most credit card issuers send you some type of correspondence indicating that they are going to send you a new or replacement card within ten days or two weeks. If it does not arrive in this time frame, it probably has been stolen. Non-receipt fraud occurs when the cards are stolen prior to delivery to the cardholder.

If your card hasn't arrived on schedule, notify the credit card issuer immediately.

Hey, don't stall—if it don't arrive, you gotta call, yeah, mon, call, don't stall, do the call, NOW!

Fraudulent Applications

Yes, these affect you, because the bad guys apply for credit cards in your good name, providing that you are creditworthy. These are false applications with mail-drop or apartment addresses where the criminals may have paid the first and last month's rent, and then use the apartment for just a few weeks to acquire, through the mail, as many credit cards as possible.

If they are using your name, this should surface when you check your credit history.

No-Card Fraud

What the heck does this mean? How can we have credit card fraud without the card? Actually without your help, no-card fraud could not happen. Yes, you have to pitch in and assist the fraudsters in defrauding yourself, or no-card fraud ain't happening. Remember those brand spoofing or phishing e-mails that you are supposed to delete? Well, if you did not delete them, and instead entered your credit card number, they now have those numbers (your numbers), and you are about to become a victim of no-card fraud. The same goes for those friendly but deceptive telemarketing phone calls where you also gave out your credit card number.

Hang up! Do not give out credit card information over the telephone to unsolicited callers; and delete those e-mails!

Counterfeit Cards

Counterfeiting equals skimming, which equals manufacturing. What this really means is that when you combine criminals and technology you get skimming. When you combine very sophisticated, computer-savvy criminals, with state of the art technology, you get a plethora of skimming methods!

Now you might ask yourself, what the heck is skimming, besides a neat word? Let me tell you that the more you research skimming, the more you wonder what the crooks are doing when they skim your card.

That black bar or stripe on the back of your credit card is called a magnetic stripe, and it contains the information that links you, the cardholder, to a particular purchase. When you make a purchase using a credit card, either the clerk swipes your card through a card reader, or you place your card into a card reader at an automated teller machine or at a gas pump. Now if we also have a little skimming going on, here is how it happens:

The clerk may have a hand-held skimming device (card reader) that captures the data in the magnetic stripe and downloads that information into their hand-held skimmer; or the ATM or gas pump card reader may have been modified by a skimming device called an *overlay* placed in the card reader. The overlay is the crook's card reader; check it out, before you put your card in, by eyeballing the card reader to make sure it looks okay. The data that was skimmed using the above methods is then downloaded onto a counterfeit credit card, and the criminals go shopping—with a counterfeit card containing your data!

First of all, remember this: skimming is the *number one* method employed by criminals to obtain your payment cards, even though they never really take your actual card; and if they do, it is only for a few seconds, and you always get your card back. Simple enough, right? Ouch, no! This is sort of a sting operation. You don't really notice anything until some time later, and then it really hurts. But it does not have to hurt at all. If you have read the book up to this point, you already know how to stop this offence and the pain of it all.

What really stings, in this sting, is that personable waiter or waitress who tells you that you are the nicest people he/she has served this week, or that overly helpful and friendly gas station clerk, who tells you that you're lookin' good, even though he's also a guy, or that sales person who says, "Hey that was *made* for little old you," is all the while skimming your card. NOW, THAT HURTS.

From everything that I have read and heard, credit card fraud is on the increase (no kidding, did it ever wane?), and technology has made skimming and counterfeit cards the number one fraudulent method employed by card fraud criminals.

"We shop, you pay!"

"We buy, you cry!"

PRICELESS!

The good news is: skimming is the one fraudulent method that you can spot and stop as soon as the criminals start using your good name. Get all of your credit cards linked up to Internet banking, and check all of the charges to your cards **daily**. Why wait for your monthly statement? This gives crooks a heck of a lot more time to whack you. Stop them dead in their tracks, just as soon as they commence these fraudulent charges. Let's use technology to **our** advantage, and make the criminals pay (or at least find some new targets). Technology is assisting the bad guys, but it also gives us a huge leg up on them. With a tiny little bit of our time, and Internet banking, we can pretty easily get this stopped. Believe me, nothing makes my day—or for that matter *yours*—like getting bad guys off the street and out of your neighbourhood before high noon. Yeah, it just doesn't get any better!

Credit cards, debit cards—clearly this is déjà-vu! What works for credit probably works for debit. The only monkey wrench thrown into the works is the personal identification number, and oh, yes, an ATM. These two things just make the crooks work harder, but never really stops them!

DEBIT CARDS

If you want to talk about something that the crooks jumped on almost from day one, look no further than the debit card and the ATM. Criminals have literally battered, bruised, and kicked the stuffing out of these two babies. (But in fact, it's hard to think of any scams or schemes that haven't already been tried and repeated a thousand times.)

Talk about a magnet—the debit card and ATM can attract bad guys with the best of them. This duo has brought almost as much attention as ladies' night at the mess! Criminals and the soon-to-be criminals absolutely love to work theft and fraud scams around ATMs and debit cards.

Now, the odd morning I get up and wonder what the actual purpose of the debit card might have been. Was it to eventually get rid of tellers, or was it a way for you to access your accounts without going to your branch? In reality, it probably was a little of each. Please don't get me wrong—the card definitely makes my life easier and certainly adds convenience; but the bad guys love it almost as much as we do. Okay, maybe even more!

Case in point: I just took a few seconds for a milk and cookie break and turned on the radio; the lead story was about the Toronto Police charging a couple following a probe into ATM skimming. Turns out the couple had used pinhole cameras (to get the personal identification number or PIN) and skimming devices in bank machines around the city, to duplicate debit cards.

Come on, let's prove to the criminals that we are not that gullible, that we are not that easy to fool; let's put a lid on this right now!

Here we go: Let me give you a debit card, and now I want you to use it, but first of all, maybe we should talk about how to keep the criminals away from it and your money. Your debit card requires a PIN; you can't use one without the other, and yes, your PIN attracts as much attention as the card.

YOUR PIN

1   All right, go ahead and choose a PIN. Pick one that you can remember, not like the cops do—believe it or not, some of the doors at police stations that have a key padlock had a code of 1111 or 2222! Trust me. Do not use numbers like these!

     Try not to use any combination of numbers that make up your personal biographical information. If you lose all of your identification, criminals like to try your house number, or date of birth, etc. If you are using some of these, they could easily work out your PIN.

2   Never write your PIN on your debit card; in fact, never write it down, period.

3.   Periodically change your PIN, two or three times a year.

4   Stop lending your debit card; you signed an agreement indicating that you would not divulge your PIN to anyone! Yes, that means spouse, father, mother, and girlfriend.

5   Use Internet banking every day to verify debit card use; be sure to notify your financial institution if you notice unauthorized debits to your account.

Okay, you have a card and a PIN. All you need now is someplace to use it. Let's start with an ATM. Come on, treat yourself today—why not withdraw forty dollars, just this once, have a nice lunch and maybe buy yourself a little something. Hey, before you get your cash, don't forget about skimming, and remember you are using a card and a PIN, which means the bad guys will need either a camera or a friendly shoulder surfer to get their hands on it.

ATMS

Let's think about this for a few minutes. If you are going to use an ATM in your neighbourhood, or around your work location, where would you feel the safest? Furthermore, is there a particular time of day that you feel better about than others? Now, I ask these questions hoping you will decide that you feel the safest at an ATM attached to a bank or a credit union. As my old Newfie staff sergeant used to say: "When all comes to all," bad guys don't usually work the safe side of the street.

Now if we can agree that an ATM at a bank or credit union is one of the safest places, let's even make it safer by using the ATM during open hours. Clearly, once the financial institution closes, it's not as safe, but it is probably still more secure than a stand-alone ATM in another location. Remember to use your free hand and/or body to shield the ATM keypad when inputting your PIN.

If you think about this skimming stuff, it's probably safe to assume that if there is skimming going on at the ATM you are about to use, the skimmers are probably somewhere close. If you see too many people standing around doing a lot of nothing, don't even bother—move on to another location.

Let me finish this part off by talking about card jams and distractions.

CARD JAMS

Some criminals prefer to jig the ATM card reader so your card will get caught and held in the reader. It sort of goes like this: your card gets stuck, and somebody offers to help you. He or she suggests that you try to input your PIN again, and if that does not work, he/she tells you to go and call the bank. Problem here is, now he has your PIN, and just as soon as you leave, he takes your card. **Do not input your PIN at the suggestion of a stranger.** Call the bank or credit union, and if necessary, the police.

DISTRACTIONS

Okay, you're standing at the ATM, card in one hand, cash in the other, receipt in the slot, and some stranger mentions that you just dropped a twenty. So you set your card down and reach for the twenty, and the stranger takes or switches your card. That old helpful helper is usually a bad guy. If you're going for his twenty, secure your card first; better still, don't get distracted.

Distraction crimes never seem to go away, and they usually happen when you're holding some money that you have just obtained from a financial institution or one of its ATMs. Do not fall for this, but when you are safely out of the area, make some notes of what happened—a description of bad guy is always good—and call the police.

Never forget, no matter what scams they pull, Internet banking will show all of the withdrawals from your accounts and charges to your credit cards. Check these daily—it takes only one little minute, and your little old daily check can immediately shut down big-league crime. And oh yes, thanks for playing detective—you may soon be up for a promotion. Keep up the good work!

We are just about to move on from payment cards, but this stuff is very important. Everybody has either had something happen to their cards, or knows somebody who had something go wrong. Criminals love these things, so stay vigilant and please do the daily detective work; or at least look at your accounts every other day.

Just before we move to the next hot items, please remember that bad guys adapt quickly, particularly those utilizing technology. There is always something new coming down the pipe. So: *update time*! Here is a new twist on the same old scam; but don't forget, although criminals are not the smartest people in the world, they count on the fact that you will not take the time to regularly check your accounts!

Here we go: You receive a telephone call from a courier company asking if you are going to be home for the next hour, as they have a delivery for you. Eventually, a man shows up at your residence with a basket of flowers and a bottle of wine (in this scam, the wine is key). Now, if you are like me, you just have to know who sent this gift. When you ask who sent the flowers and wine, the courier guy says, "I'm just delivering the gift—the card is being sent separately."

This should start your fraud meter ticking a bit, because it is a little odd—although not over the top—but now I'm thinking that maybe we are starting down that old fraudulent path. Next, the individual indicates that because the gift contains alcohol, he has to charge you $3.50 as proof that he has delivered to an adult. This part is believable; surely we do not want alcohol left on the porch. When you reach for your cash, courier man says the company requires payment by EFTPOS (electronic funds transfer at point of sale). This way he is not handling cash, and everything is accounted for. Seems reasonable, but I'm still not going to use my payment cards.

At this point, courier man pulls out a small, hand-held, mobile device, with a screen to enter a PIN. You then take one of your payment cards, enter your PIN, and a receipt is printed out. The fraudster now has your card number and PIN stored in his handy little machine.

How many people are going to get caught in this scam? Okay, those of you who read the book will be home free, I HOPE! But the rest, ouch!

What the heck is going on here:

- We have been offered something for nothing, or almost nothing.

- It is a gift that attracts—we all love flowers and wine.

- It is an unsolicited gift.

- We do not know whom it is from.

- We are talking to a guy we do not know.

- He cannot (will not) take cash.

Kinda has a smell of fraud . . . yes, you could tell yourself it's probably from my sweetie, Reggie. But come on, after twenty-one years of marriage, he's still taking you to Burger King. Just keep doing that old Internet banking review, and you're going to be all right.

Gals, this next paragraph is not really important—it's a little something I remembered from the flower part, so just skip over it and go on to the next one.

Okay, guys, listen up, this is a bit of friendly guy talk, but make sure we keep this amongst ourselves. Some time back, I was working in a small office with a woman who was separated from her partner. It was Valentine's Day. Yeah, gotta love it. Anyway, at approximately nine-thirty a.m., she received a dozen beautiful red roses from her ex. She promptly stood up walked over to me, threw the roses on my desk, and told me to get rid of them! Now, I wanted to give her one of the roses, but I also wanted to live, so at about ten a.m., I decided to go around the building and give one rose to twelve different folks—you know, guys, Nicole, Elizabeth, Geri, Julie, Yvonne, Monica, Candy, etc. To my amazement, when I walked into an office and wished a happy V Day, these people jumped up, ran around or over their desks, and gave me multiple hugs and kisses.

Now, I never thought of this as fraudulent, but when word spread about how I had obtained the roses and how many people I had given a rose to, suffice it to say that by 10:10 a.m., they were hunting me down.

Just a long way of saying an inducement like a gift of flowers, or even a flower, elicits a hell of a positive reaction. Flower power is clearly a great facilitator for fraud; it seems to be very difficult for anyone to show ill will to the bearer of a gift of flowers!

Hey, gals, be careful out there—always be leery of unknown people bearing gifts that we all love—you know, those romantic-type things. This is just a heads-up: assume nothing! They may be pulling an end run!

REAL ESTATE FRAUD
(MORTGAGE AND TITLE FRAUD)

After all those years of saving, scrimping, making sacrifices, you now have your own home, cottage, or condo—the ultimate big-ticket family item . . . no more renting . . . this is as good as it gets. The whole crew under one roof, and at the end of the day, you got the mortgage paid off, and the place is yours! Okay so the property taxes might almost equal your original mortgage payments, but the place is yours, no more mortgage—you hope!

Mortgage fraud is as sickening as it gets, and it is prevalent because it nets criminals very large sums of money in one small scam. The sad part is the fact that many of the low-lifes who commit this stuff seem to be back on the street before you can get this mess worked through. The financial institution gets scammed, the lawyers get scammed, and you get another mortgage that you never applied for and never knew about until a monthly statement arrives. The crooks have all of the money, and you have another mortgage!

This is a very lucrative and unique type of fraud, because the fraud is not perpetrated against you as an individual; this type of identity fraud is perpetrated directly against a financial institution, and they suffer the initial loss. But although the loss is initially on the books of the financial institution, it eventually finds its way into your residence in the form of a mortgage on your property!

Mortgage fraud requires four definitive things:

- A fraudster
- A land title/registry office
- A financial institution
- Your photo identification

LAND REGISTRY OFFICES

No matter where you live—city, region, or county—there will be a government office in the area that keeps records of property ownership. The land registry office registers, stores, and manages all deeds and mortgages.

The following information is available from the above-mentioned office:

- Name or names of the property owner(s) (who's on title)

- All mortgages registered on title

- All transactions, including sales and transfers

- Liens registered on title

The tricky part about the land registry office is that fact that the records are in the public domain. This means that virtually anyone can go to any registry office, pay a small fee, and obtain all of the information on your property. Yes, this is a windfall for criminals, because they can obtain the full names of the property owners, the amounts of any mortgages registered against title, and the name of the institution that provided the mortgage.

Okay, let's huddle up for a minute . . . everybody take a deep breath, count to ten . . . hey, *slowly* count to ten . . . now, let's talk! People, people, look I know this sucks, but go ahead and yell a bit more anyway . . . and yes, I realize that some days there may be as many bad guys as law clerks at the land registry office, and yes, this isn't fair, but welcome to reality. Real-estate fraud is very similar to real estate, in that the important things are location and credit worthiness. Location does not matter if you have bad credit, because I probably cannot legally acquire a mortgage in your name, so I have to find another target. So now you realize how criminals get some of your vital information: they do not have to take your garbage or steal your mail; they just have to find the land registry office, and *bingo,* they have a whole lot of useful and valuable information.

Now, I probably shouldn't mention this, but most financial institutions, lawyer's offices, and real-estate offices have an on-line system called "Teraview," which allows these groups to do searches without leaving their offices. The bad guys can either go to the land registry office or utilize Teraview to find out who is on title, if there are any mortgages, which institution holds the mortgage, and the original amount of the mortgage. That's a huge *ouch*.

Now, the criminals have some options:

- They can discharge any existing mortgages (utilizing fraudulent documentation).

- They can switch the title on the property.

- They can sell the property.

- They can obtain a mortgage on the property.

FINANCIAL INSTITUTION (F.I.)

The bad guys already know where you obtained your current mortgage, so they are probably heading to another F.I. to acquire mortgage funds for your property.

They also know that they require photo identification, and one or two other pieces of identification in your name.

Photo identification is a driver's licence or a passport. Most criminals produce a driver's licence with *their* photograph and *your* information. The police refer to this as a "genuine altered driver's licence," because it is usually completed on an actual provincial or state blank driver's licence.

Now just one more piece of identification, and they are ready to be you.

Remember that the only reason for crooks to become involved in real-estate fraud, whether they switch title or not, is to eventually place a new mortgage on your home and take the proceeds. The criminals, armed with photo identification in your name and the information they gleaned from the land registry records, enter a financial institution *as you*, and make a mortgage application for your property. They could also apply for a line of credit using your residence as collateral. This usually ends with the financial institution's getting stung, and some serious money being taken by somebody who said they were you! And very soon you will receive a statement indicating the amount of your new mortgage, or line of credit, and the amount of your monthly payments.

I should also mention that if you own rental property, your tenants could pull some fancy tricks. Some tenants have switched the title to their name, and then sold the property. Some other enterprising tenants have also listed the premises for rent, collected the first and last month's rent from a number of new tenants, and then left town!

PROTECT YOUR PROPERTY

If you have read the book up to this point, I know you have been checking your credit history to ensure that there are no enquiries from financial institutions to which you have not applied for credit. Further, you now know that you can also periodically check your title. A lawyer can check your title for you, or better still, you can do it yourself. If the criminals can hang out at the land registry office, so can you!

We can probably agree that insurance in any form is a good thing. Nothing like additional protection, and some peace of mind, to help out if something goes wrong. Yes, it is time to consider **title insurance**—something that will defend your title if bad guys are tampering with it. When most of us purchased property, the lawyer acting for us likely included title insurance as part of the transaction. This type of title insurance was in place to offer assistance up to the purchase date, in case there was a legal problem (e.g., defects in the title that may have been created in the past). This traditional type of title insurance might not defend your title if anything happens *after* the purchase date.

Now, what do you do?

First, check to see if you already have title insurance.

Next, make sure it protects your title *after* the purchase date. This is usually called "existing homeowner's title insurance," and it defends your title for as long as you own your home.

If you do not have existing homeowner's title insurance, get it! It is very inexpensive protection for your property, and normally involves just a one-time fee for as long as you own your property.

Quick recap: Check your credit history; check your title; purchase existing homeowner's title insurance.

If you are considering purchasing a new or older home, take some **precautions**:

- Make sure the seller is also the person on title.

- Ensure that the home has not been flipped several times in a short time frame. There are many homes that have been purchased by criminals, then sold to complicit individuals a few times over a short time frame in order to artificially inflate the price of the home.

- Do your homework when purchasing a resale home—you do not want to purchase a former marijuana grow-op! Check with the town or city clerk's office or the local police, or search the old newspaper section of your library.

9: BECOMING A SENIOR

Here are some thoughts and musings based on interacting with the public at large during my twenty-six years as a member of the RCMP.

Life as I see it: One day you show up in this good old world, a little baby, and all you need is somebody to feed you, change your diaper, and put you back in the cradle.

Eventually they force you out of the house on a daily basis, and put you in school. During this time, you somehow become interested in the opposite sex! You start working; you somehow become *very* interested in the opposite sex! You leave the family nest, and get your own place. With your own place you somehow become *extremely* interested in the opposite sex. Hopefully after a lot of searching, trial and error, you find Miss or Mister RIGHT.

Yes, you get married, you have some kids; you become Mom and Dad. You spend the next twenty years at swimming lessons, ballet, baseball, hockey, tennis, art class, gymnastics, golf lessons, and so on, while trying to save some money for the kids' university tuition.

Finally, the last kid leaves home, and you guys are right back where you started. But wait a minute—kids keep coming back to borrow money, your car, your food; even for the odd sleepover.

Believe me, I know; it seems like yesterday when you were only fifty—what happened? Hello, you're now a SENIOR! What next?

You are not alone; seniors represent one of the fastest-growing groups within Canada, and for reasons I have not quite figured out, as we age, the gals certainly seem to outlast the guys!

Constable Karen Burnell, a veteran member of the Royal Canadian Mounted Police, always emphasized three things when she spoke to groups of seniors:

- If anyone offers you a free prize, then free means free. Do not send anyone money, or pay any fee to claim a free prize.

- Never give out your social insurance number, credit card numbers, or bank information to random individuals who telephone you, knock at your door, or send you something in the mail.

- Never forget that criminals have worked advance-fee schemes forever. Do not pay for goods or services beforehand.

Cst. Burnell also mentioned that most seniors are very trusting; as a result, they might be easily swayed by someone who seems genuine and very friendly. Remember, before you make any decisions that involve your personal finances, talk it over with a relative, friend, or someone else that you trust.

Seniors may not necessarily contact the police if they become victims of crime, because they feel embarrassed. Hey, make sure you make the call! We all make mistakes—believe me, you are not alone.

After having read the book to this point, you already have an inkling that certain lowlife criminals target seniors; they keep using the same old scams and schemes because these senior scams keep working!

All right, no matter what, read the next part, because I'm going to describe the main scams and how they work. Remember: To be able to harm you, or at least harm your finances, they have to communicate with you, and you then have to do something, and that something will usually do you in. As I have said many times in this book, stop helping the bad guys get their hands on your money! They simply cannot grab your money without your handing it to them, or giving them the information they need to find it.

TIP#14: If anyone comes to your front door, or telephones you, and this is a random, unsolicited call or knock, hang up, close the door . . . keep your hard-earned money in your own pocket.

MAIN SCAMS AND HOW THEY WORK

THE TELEPHONE

Could anyone survive without a telephone? Maybe, but only for a very few minutes. A telephone is essential; just think about your life without a phone. But remember, the telephone is one of the main tools utilized by the bad guys to help them obtain a free pass to your money.

Let's do a practice round: Unsolicited call comes in . . . criminal starts talking . . . first thing you do? Yes, *hang up*!

Let me give you some examples:

- Caller says you have won a contest; you're a big prize winner, but to get the prize, you have to pay some type of fee. (Hey, don't forget, you never really *entered* this contest in the first place.)

- Caller says this is your opportunity to get in on the ground floor of a huge investment with a really huge return. But you must act today—do not miss out—this is a limited-time offer. Caller then asks for personal or banking and credit card information. Remember, you are talking to someone you do not know, someone who randomly called you and is trying to pressure you. What next? Yes, *just hang up*!

- Caller claims to be a lawyer, a police officer, a bank inspector, a government official . . . if he or she wants financial information, just hang up. Don't forget, they called you.

Once you start answering questions that are financial, life style, or personal in nature, and you are speaking with a criminal telemarketer, they keep a book on you; they sometimes call back four or five times a day. Let's get this stopped. Yes, I mean *stopped right now*. Never give any information to unsolicited telephone callers. Don't put yourself on the hook. All random callers get the same response: a polite goodbye followed by an immediate disconnect.

Remember, every day between nine a.m. and four p.m., or any other time criminal telemarketers believe that seniors are home alone, they start calling. The only reason to call is to scam you out of your money, so they come up with a lot of something for nothing, add a sense of urgency, and offer huge returns, and this is all wrapped up in something that they think will make you want to get on board—things like promotions for lottery tickets, big prizes, charitable donations, and every type of investment opportunity that you can think of. HANG UP.

I hate to bring this up, but you're over fifty-five, you have by now been out and about one heck of a long time. Other than your good old mom giving you some money, how many times did anyone else you did not know—anyone who just selected you at random—offer you a legitimate opportunity to get rich?

Ouch! We both know that the way life seems to work is that if someone has some way to make a ton of dough, they ain't sharing! It just doesn't happen. There simply is no quick way to get rich through scams and schemes that guarantee you will make a small fortune, or get a beautiful massive prize. What the heck, don't even bother answering the phone during the day!

YOUR FRONT DOOR

The next knock you hear may be some overly friendly, overly helpful type posing as a home renovations person—someone whom you do not know, someone who "just happened to be in your neighbourhood," and selected you at random. Now, you have been able to fight these guys off on the telephone, so make sure you do not get whacked at the front door!

Home repair fraud can happen to anyone, but these criminals appear to target seniors. Good news is, they use a lot of the

- In the event of a Public Utility inspection, do not let these individuals into your home until you verify with the utility that they are in fact their employees and you find out the reason for their visit.

- If someone knocks on your door and asks to use the washroom or telephone, **say NO.**

- In the event of a charity solicitation, it is good to give some money to help others if you are able, but pick your own charity. Do not get pressured at the door or on the telephone. Your own church can probably use some extra money, and you can bet your seniors group needs it; you decide. Stay with organizations that you know, not those that try to pressure you.

Remember, seniors are targeted by criminals, and seniors widowed and living alone get even more attention from the bad guys. Never let unsolicited callers or those who appear at your door know anything about your personal life. In fact, tell them to keep it down a bit, because the police officer that you rent a room to is trying to sleep!

MAIL

All of the offers you receive by telephone or at the front door also show up in your mailbox. If you have never heard of the company, or the offer is just too good to be true, put it in File 13—that's the garbage!

SOME SAFETY TOOLS AND TIPS

CELLULAR TELEPHONE

Please tell me you have one! In many ways, this little gadget is your lifeline. You do not need a fancy one—just get something that works well, and get a "pay as you go" plan. Remember, this cell phone is just for emergencies. Take it with you when you are out of the house—yes, don't leave home without it!

same scams over and over. Keeping in mind that you are probably the one person who knows if something at your residence needs repair, be very leery of anyone stating the following:

- We are working in your neighbourhood.

- I noticed that your roof . . . brickwork . . . driveway . . . chimney, etc., needs repair (anything that they can see from the street).

- Because we already have our equipment here, we can give you a special price.

- Because of your age, you also qualify for a senior's discount.

- We have some left-over material from our last job.

All of the above leads to your being pressured to sign a contract *immediately* to take advantage of the deep discounts. Next, they will want a substantial down payment. STOP right here! This is starting to smell like fraud.

If your home needs repairs, deal with established companies and get a couple of estimates. If anyone pressures you, move on. In many of the home repair frauds I have investigated, I was not able to find the actual company; the address was a mail drop. I could not find the company listed at the provincial company's branch, the telephone numbers were all for cellular phones, and there was no telephone listing for the company. Oh yes, these investigations were all a result of door-to-door solicitations.

Under no circumstances should you let these people into your residence to see what else needs repair. They might be criminals. Keep them outside.

Let's have a quick recap:

- If anyone calls to ask for your help in a bank or police/ bank investigation, HANG UP. It's not the police or your bank that's calling—it's just another criminal.

- For all home repairs, get three estimates; use established companies.

Home Alarm System

If set up properly, this can also be another lifesaver, particularly if something happens to you inside of your residence. When we think of home alarms, we think of break-ins, but these systems go way beyond just protecting your property from criminals. Many systems come with a portable alarm button that you can carry on your person, and if you fall or get hurt, you can just press the button. Some systems have voice communication, allowing you to speak with someone at the alarm station. This way, you know they have received the alarm and are aware of your problem.

One of the really great features of some systems is that you can have your smoke detectors hooked into the alarm system. This allows the alarm company to notify the fire department, whether you are at home or not. Some systems also monitor carbon monoxide levels and monitor basement temperature to alert you if the temperature is getting low enough to cause pipes to freeze.

Let me talk for a moment about break-ins. Many residential break-ins occur during the daylight hours, a time when criminals believe no one is home. A lot of the time, bad guys enter the residence through the back of the home, or through the side door of the garage. Patio doors or sliding glass doors are a favourite entry point from the back of the house; basement windows are sometimes entered.

Many night break-ins are for the purpose of stealing your vehicle. There is a belief that many people leave their car keys sitting on a hook or on a table by an entrance door. It does not take long to force a door, grab the car keys, and drive off; maybe you need to move your car keys to another location.

Believe it or not, signs do deter criminals. During daylight, the bad guys will ring your doorbell, and if no one answers, they will go to the backyard and break in. A sign on the front door is a good thing. Place a decal from your alarm company on the door and consider some of the following:

• Beware of dog.

• Dog is not chained.

- Police officer working shifts sleeping—do not ring doorbell (officer is a very light sleeper).

- No trespassing.

- Trespassers will be prosecuted.

Remember: at night, random people cannot come onto your property.

YOUR CAR

Just some pointers to keep you safer:

- Do not leave the keys in the ignition, or leave your vehicle running, even if you are only out of the vehicle for a few seconds.

- In the winter, do not leave your vehicle unattended and warming up in the driveway.

- Do not leave anything in plain view inside of your vehicle; place all items of value in your locked trunk.

- If you are parking and leaving your vehicle unattended, take your insurance certificate and the vehicle ownership with you.

- When returning to your vehicle, make sure no one is in your vehicle before you unlock the door.

- When purchasing fuel at a service station, utilize a speed pass or Ez-Pay[2] instead of using a credit card or cash.

We have all heard the term "carjacking." One type of carjacking that you must be aware of involves your vehicle's being bumped from behind, usually just a light bump. But when you get out of your car to check the damage, your car is taken. If your vehicle is bumped, do not get out of your car. Keep your doors locked. Assess the situation. If you feel threatened, get your cell phone out and call 9-1-1.

---

2   This is a symbol on the pump that you simply need to touch; the company already has your credit card information, and your account will automatically be debited in the amount of your purchase.

PERSONAL SAFETY

- It's always a good idea to check in with a friend or relative daily; so every day at the same time, say, ten a.m., telephone the same person, let him or her know that everything is kosher, and if you have any travel plans for that day, let her/him know where you are going.

- Use only one initial and your last name on personal cheques, apartment or condo directories, and the telephone book.

- If you live alone, consider putting another name alongside yours. Do not let strangers know that you are widowed or living alone.

- If you need cash, and are using an ATM, do it during open hours at a financial institution.

TELEPHONE — LONG DISTANCE (IS IT FREE?)

At this point in time, calls to the following telephone numbers can be made without paying a long distance charge. These toll-free telephone numbers start with the following area codes: 1–800, 1–877, and 1–888.

Telephone charges to the following area codes are **not free**. First and foremost, the 1–900: this means $$$$, usually a minimum of $35.00 per call. You can also add the following area codes: 1–976 and 1–809; calls to these area codes will result in a charge being added to your monthly telephone bill! Let me tell you this: People have contacted me and said that charges of $35.00 and $50.00 had been listed on their monthly phone bills when they called the above area codes. I have been told that some fees can go even higher. Hey, be careful, out there — watch whom you are calling!

Okay, everybody, time out for a minute; let's take a moment to contemplate the most important parts of this chapter. Let me give you the bottom line on what you need to remember more than anything else. **Criminals in the form of telemarketers, or door-to-door home renovation people, cannot ever**

defraud you if you don't give them the information they need to do it.

Bottom line, just one more time: Stop communicating personal and financial information to people who call you on the telephone at random. Stop answering the doorbell and giving out personal and financial information to individuals who appear at your door with great but urgent home renovation deals. STOP falling for those get-rich-quick schemes! The only person getting rich is the person you are dealing with.

If someone posing as a salesperson comes knocking and indicates that you need some home repairs, do not get caught up in the old urgent "you must sign a contract today to take advantage of these great discount offers." Never let these individuals into your home to conduct a survey, or for any other reason. Always utilize known, established contractors and obtain at least two estimates before you decide on whom you're going to hire, and yes, get a contract. At the end of the day, we can stop these scams.

When you look at the police statistics, there is a disproportionate number of seniors who get caught up in telemarketing, home renovation, and charitable donation scams and schemes. Never forget: if these people find out you're a widow or widower, then they become relentless in the pursuit of your money.

You've got a lot of life experience behind you, and yes, you actually know that you cannot get that two-week vacation in Florida if you buy twenty-five pens for twenty-five dollars. You know that if someone tells you that you have won a fabulous prize in a contest you never entered, this is quickly going down the slippery fraud slope. At the same time, I realize that if you have the ability, you may want to help others; but do not get caught up in any charitable donation scams, no matter how desperate they make the situation appear. Believe me, you and I both know that your local seniors' group or your church or service organization also needs help and, in fact, one of these groups might be sending money to the cause you are being harassed by.

A few months ago, I was conducting a neighbourhood investigation, and when this one senior individual opened his front door, I panicked a bit—not because he wasn't courteous, but because

I could hear what sounded like two Dobermans and a pit-bull barking in the rear of the house. Once I had identified myself and we spoke for a moment, he indicated that the barking was simply a recording. I must say, the sound of barking, along with his sign on the front door that stated BEWARE DOG NOT CHAINED, was extremely effective.

When you pick up your mail, or you get a telephone call, or you receive an e-mail, or somebody rings the doorbell, with offers that involve your receiving large sums of money, huge gifts, or vacations; or solicitations for charitable donations, home renovations, or lottery pools, do the following:

- Just say, "No thank you."

- Do not answer personal questions.

- Never give out financial information.

- Do not let anyone into your home for any reason.

- Do not let anyone know you live alone.

JUST SAY NO!

If you believe something is legitimate, before you do anything, do the following:

- Discuss it with a relative.

- Talk to the manager of your financial institution.

- Talk to someone at your seniors' association or your church.

Never forget that we all need help and advice sometimes. Two heads are better than one, and it's better to get an expert opinion than to get caught up in fraud.

A lot of the things I have mentioned are just common sense. We live in one of the safest countries in the world, so it's okay to enjoy life and get out and do things. But be safe, be careful out there, and yes, have a lot of fun—you've earned it.

More Social Philosophy

For what it's worth, I would like to share some more observations that have stayed with me as a result of interacting with people.

Let me start with the good old family—Mom, Dad, and all of the kids. Yes, eventually the kids hopefully leave the nest . . . okay, some may move back in for a while, but hey, we're family; no big deal. But sometimes along the way, life happens—disagreements, arguments, things are said in the heat of the moment, and as a result, we have some members of some families not speaking to each other. On two separate occasions I have had to attend at homes and inform families that Mom or Dad, or sister or brother, had been killed. This is devastating enough, but imagine the anguish when some member of the family was not on speaking terms with the deceased.

At funerals, people have mentioned to me that they had not spoken to their daughter in over three years; or son or daughter have mentioned that they had not spoken with parents for years—and now, regretfully, it's too late.

Let me say this: If you do not have a normal relationship with your family members, you will regret it for as long as you live. Now we have come to the tough part. You have to be the bigger person; you need to contact the family members that you have not spoken to in some time. Yes, you can send a note; better still, you can leave a voice message—just a matter of telling them you care and you miss them. Maybe you can invite them to come over to the house at their leisure. But step up, bury the hatchet, forget the past. Life is too short, and it never gets any better than communicating with all family members. Remember, do not bring up (and I mean never bring up) the old problems. Move on. You might even tell them you love them—it will make their life better, and it will most definitely enhance your life, Big Time.

And another thing, what about a couple of family dinners, other than at the holidays? Maybe a summer picnic, and a nice fall dinner. Gosh, I can still taste Mom's roast beef and her gravy; nobody did it better. And yes, good old Mom prepared the same meal every Sunday evening; believe me, nobody missed Sunday dinner! Did I mention back bacon and eggs, every Sunday after church, to die for? As seniors, you already know life's too short, so take the time to have frequent family get-togethers; they certainly make for great memories. They are also very good for the soul.

SAFETY, SECURITY, AND ENJOYMENT

Okay, what's up with some of the clothes you guys are wearing? Those pants, shoes, and winter hats—are those things really hats? Let me give you a hand up, there is absolutely nothing more comfortable to walk around in than athletic or training shoes; you hardly know you have shoes on. Get yourself a nice pair of Nike athletic shoes, and while you're there, grab a nice Nike toque and a training or warm-up suit. Believe me, this is as comfortable as it gets; never mind how sharp you look!

Now that you have that Nike gear, let's put it to good use. When you finally retire, it's not necessarily the job you miss, but most of the people . . . all the kibitzing, all the one-liners . . . In the RCMP there were some great one-liners. If you showed up with a fresh haircut, somebody would say, "You better start tipping the barber"; or a new jacket, "Did you get that free with a filler up?" Yup, you miss that.

Now, you're sitting at home in the morning, reading and looking at four walls. (By the way it's okay if you're reading my book!) But let's do something very positive, let's start our day at the local fitness club, gym, or health club. Hey, hey, doesn't matter if you have never worked out before! With that new Nike gear you sure look like you belong here. Just sit on a bike and do some slow pedalling. Take a look around and see what everyone else is doing. See, already two people have said good morning to you!

Yes, the good old gym . . . between nine a.m. and eleven-thirty a.m., Monday to Friday, you have a lot of retirees, a lot of housewives, and a lot of seniors. It is a very pleasant and friendly environment at this time of the morning. Pretty soon, you will have some friends, the one-liners will start, and the kibitzing. Some people even discuss the Leafs in the morning! Start slow, do some aerobic stuff, and then start some weight training, but remember: everybody here started at your level. This is a great healthy, social, and very positive way to start your day. Hey, what else could you do for one hour a day that brings this type of benefit to your mind and body and at the same time enhances your quality of life? JUST DO IT!

10: SOME THINGS YOU NEED TO KNOW ABOUT TECHNOLOGY

The blackberry, the ipod, Bluetooth, smart phones, MP3 players, wireless web, global positioning system (GPS), GPS tracking device . . . **holy technological tussle, Batman!**

Yes, yes, Robin, it's an absolute nightmare. Regrettably, we may have to return to college for a number of years if we intend to continue fighting crime in the new millennium. Hold on . . . I have an idea . . . yes, Batman, we could purchase a wireless router, some graphic cards, a DVD burner, a motherboard, RAM, a USB drive—

Sorry, Robin, I quit!

Holy teamwork, Batman!

But Robin, I'm still trying to program my VCR!

Holy cow! Are the crime fighters quitting, are the bad guys winning, are we all playing catch-up? It's probably a little of each. **One thing that we do know is that almost every new technological advancement and every upgrade to that new technology brings new opportunities to criminals.** Advancing technology attracts the criminals, and it certainly gives them a lot more tools for defrauding you, particularly when they never require any face-to-face interaction with those they target. In fact, you might be just one more e-mail or text message away from them.

At this point in the book, we already know that when the bad guys can work some form of criminal activity against you, and never have to deal with you in person, never any face to face, they become a lot more aggressive.

You are not **alone,** when you consider there are software programs that allow me to see from my computer if your car is still in your driveway, or to see if you are at your mother's house, or almost anywhere else you said you were going. You truly are not alone anymore—particularly if you are married to or dating a very jealous person, a very controlling person, or the wrong person (they might all be the same person). I can simply leave my cell phone, equipped with some type of GPS feature, under the seat of your car and track wherever you have been. With all of the various GPS systems and related software programs, anyone can find out a lot about you, without ever leaving his or her computer!

So you've got that up-to-date, do-everything cell phone, or the can't-live-without Barack berry—sorry, blackberry. Yes, if it's good enough for a Harvard law school grad, it's good enough for you. All of you cell phone and blackberry lovers—and that's a heck of a lot of us—tell me this: what kind of information do you have stored in your cell? I only ask this because a friend of mine told me that her car was broken into, and her cell phone was stolen. Okay, I didn't want to ask her this question, but I did wonder how the heck she could leave her cell in her car—holy asking for a break-in! The frightening thing was the stuff she had stored in her phone: bank account numbers, access codes, photos, telephone numbers, addresses, etc. This is at least as good as stealing your purse or wallet.

So, What Can Happen?

A gal had her handbag stolen from her office, sometime after lunch. The handbag had her wallet, cash, credit cards, debit card, and cell phone. When she discovered the loss, she immediately called her husband, who said: "I got your text message about our joint bank account. I sent you the PIN—you can never remember it."

"My God, I lost my purse, and my cell phone was in it!"

"Holy—call the bank!"

Yes, the thief had used her cell to text a person on her contact list; he sent a text to the name "honey bunny," asking for the PIN for their chequing account. Unfortunately, honey bunny texted the PIN back to his wife's cell—which was now in the hands of the bad guy. He had her cell, her PIN, and her debit card; of course, he started withdrawing their cash!

Now you all know that I sure don't want to tell you how to live your life, but let me give you a few suggestions. On your cell contact list, avoid using names that identify a person's relationship to you. Names like, sweet pea, hot chick, hunky, hubby, dad, mom, cupcake, iron man, boo, puddin' . . . you get my drift.

If you receive a text message regarding confidential or personal information, make a call (you are holding a cell) to the sender to confirm it is really that person before you send the info! Also please remember that your text message might not be deleted for a long time, so be very careful about sending personal and financial information to *anyone*. The same thing applies to text messages or e-mails from friends or family about meeting up at a particular location; make a call to confirm the meeting is legit.

Your Car

Let's talk for a minute about your **automobile**, or more specifically where you park it when away from home. Three things to think about:

1   Your garage door opener = key to your house.

2   Your GPS = finding your residence.

3.   Your ownership and insurance = your address.

Now think about this: do I really need anything else to do you serious harm? These three things are all I really need. At this point in time, I am only missing one thing: your whereabouts; once I determine where you are, I have a time frame to work with. So what's next . . . I may set up at commuter parking lots, transit lots, sporting events, anywhere that I can determine that you and your significant other are together. Now I just have to decide how long you are going to be away, and then go and check out your house.

So, the bad guys know how far you are from home, they have some idea of how long you are going to be away, and you were kind enough to leave them all the tools they need to clean out your residence. My guess is that they will probably have a rather **large** truck, when they eventually get to your home!

Just think about how much crime we could stop, if we took the time (it's not really a lot of time) to make it extremely difficult for bad guys to get their hands on our property. Over the years, I have spent a lot of time with victims of crime, and although I have never told them this, a lot of victims were the authors of their own misfortune. They clearly, although unwittingly, helped the criminals. If you keep leaving them enough really good clues, they will not remain clueless for long!

Somebody please tell me what the heck ever happened to **pay phones** and **pagers.**

11: HEY, SOME MORE KINDS OF GOOD OLD FRAUD

And yes, these have been around forever, just some new twists and back at you, because you keep falling for the same old stuff, so it never really gets old. Yeah, what's old is suddenly new again and again and again, thanks to you!

CHEQUES

Or not enough CHECKING—aka, DIGGING YOUR OWN GRAVE.

Let me commence this chapter with the words of Sergeant Ron Belanger, RCMP veteran member: "Cheque fraud—two simple words . . . with the ability to rob you of your wealth and destroy your reputation."

CHEQUE FRAUD

Cheque fraud is one of the fastest growing financial crimes in Canada. Several large accounting firms have estimated annual losses in North America to exceed twenty billion dollars, of which we have more than our fair share here in Canada. It is projected that fraud losses due to forged cheques will increase twenty-five percent each year.

There are many different fraudulent schemes involving phony cheques. The number of stolen, altered, and counterfeit cheques in circulation has reached near epidemic proportions. Cheque fraud continues to plague businesses and individuals, often to the point of financial ruination.

I think I remember a time when we all made our payments with cheques, or on payday when your employer handed you a cheque. But a lot of us have gotten away from paying for things with personal cheques, instead paying with direct deposits, Internet banking, and credit cards. We do not seem to utilize the cheque book much anymore.

We have all heard, "The cheque's in the mail," or "His cheque bounced." So what's up with cheques? Actually they have become an immense problem, not the cheques themselves that are sent out for lawful purposes, but the cheques that are either stolen from the mail, stolen from your briefcase or purse, or taken during break-ins. Cheques that already have a payee get altered, and blank cheques get forged and/or counterfeited.

Having read the preceding chapters, you will know that when you deal with individuals whom you have never met, do not know, have no idea of where they actually live, and have no face-to-face contact with them, it can quickly lead to fraud! Yes, imagine getting up one morning, grabbing the mail, and finding a cheque for three, four, or even five thousand dollars. Remember that it's not Christmas, the cheque is not from your good old mom, it's not a little something from sweet old Grandma . . . it's four thousand dollars from somebody you do not know, have never met, and never heard of. Hey, is this normal? Has it ever happened before? If you think this is cool, I need to step outside for a minute and take a deep breath, and so do you! Please tell me when was the last time you sent out a bunch of cheques worth thousands of dollars to people you did not know. I'm hoping, praying, the answer is never! *This is some sort of fraud.*

Now, what really gets mystifying in this type of cheque fraud is the fact that the bad guys want little old you to deposit the cheque. You are to keep a little bit for yourself and wire transfer or send one of your own personal cheques in the amount of almost all of the funds they sent to you to another place or person. Okay . . . let me get this straight: they send you a cheque, but you are supposed to send most of the money somewhere else! *This is fraud!* Nobody does this sort of thing except criminals. They are hoping that for the promise of a few bucks, you will be crazy enough to deposit the cheque into your own personal account and then send the money back to them, or to accounts that they control. OUCH.

Of course, there is always a little twist to this; for instance, your cheque may be attached to a letter indicating that you have won several thousand dollars, and you just have to wire the proceeds of this little cheque back, and then someday the thousands will arrive. Don't hold your breath! Or you have won a lottery prize or an expensive trip, and you just need to deposit the cheque and send the proceeds back.

Just send their cheque back. This is fraud.

Reputable, long-standing corporations that issue free prizes, free vacations, free stuff, or free whatever, do not charge you a fee to collect your *free* prize!

IF SOMEONE PAYS YOU WITH A BAD CHEQUE

Okay, so what happens if you go ahead and deposit a fraudulent or counterfeit cheque into your bank account? First, the bank credits your account with the amount of the cheque; then your bank sends (clears) the cheque back to the paying bank for payment. The paying bank then debits their customer's account, and the cheque eventually is sent back to their customer. The cheque could go back to the customer in a couple of days, or a couple of weeks, and when received by the customer it may not be looked at for a couple of days or a couple of weeks. Now the customer looks at the cheque and says, holy moly, this is counterfeit, and rushes back to his bank. They then send the cheque back to the bank where you originally deposited the cheque, as a fraudulent item. Your bank then debits your own personal account for the amount of the deposit. Oh sorry, I should have mentioned that all of this gets compounded if the paying bank is in another country—it adds a lot more days to the process, and gives the criminals more time to work you over before your bank tells you that the cheque you deposited was counterfeit!

Like most forms of fraud, cheque fraud always starts with your receiving something that appears to have value, something that makes you see dollar signs. Bear in mind that cheque fraud cannot happen, can never get off the ground, can absolutely never harm you or your finances—unless you accept that good

old cheque, knowing deep down that this cheque is problem-
atic, and do something very silly with it. Yes, if you never deposit
that cheque, you will be fine; fraud cannot happen. Period.
Sure, I already know that if I come out to your home to investigate, you're going to tell me that you were positive that you
had won thousands in a lottery that you had never entered; that
your deceased distant uncle Lester, now known as Very Lucky
Lester, of whom up until now you had never heard, left you a
small fortune; or that somebody you have never met, and still
do not know, trusted you to collect thousands in cheques for
them.

Please, we are smarter than the criminals—somebody please
tell me that we are—nobody just ups and sends you a cheque for
no good reason. If they do, IT'S COUNTERFEIT. Methinks it's time
for you to save your own bacon, stop dreaming, stop believing
in fairy tales! Who the heck do you think goes around sending
around free money? No one but a criminal sends out cheques
for no reason. Why would they send you a cheque to send back?
Why don't they just send the money themselves? Why do they
need you in the middle? Let's face it: there are no free rides; there
is no free money! I think P.T. Barnum of the Barnum and Bailey
Circus once said there is a sucker born every minute. Please,
please, stop proving him right.

Let me see . . . okay, it's a little after six p.m. Why don't we all put
the book down for a while, and go get a bite to eat? I'm just going
to head over to Horton's, grab a chili and of course a double
chocolate donut; be back in an hour, hour and a half.

Hey, I'm back, and look what I found . . . had my dinner and
thought I would send Mom an e-mail, and look what was in my
inbox.

■ ■ ■

Technology Industry Park, Luqiao, Taizhou,
Zhejiang, China 318050

We are a stock-share enterprise, whose major products
are SanOu and Harvest-brand power tool accessories and
CNC machining center accessories, which are exported to

other companies/concerns especially in Europe, America, Asia and Canada.

We are offering international clients financial management services, we are searching for representatives who can help us establish a medium of getting to our customers, It will be a part-time and highly-paid job from home, with no downpayment, no investments, no special knowlege and skills. We do need trustable and serious partners in the afformentioned countries, with the following specicifications - Age 22+ and above -2-3 times a day Internet access -3-4 hours per WEEK, -Work from home. Business (LLC or S-Corp) owners are welcome. We can offer great opportunity for your business.

Average income will 10% of any transaction or funds received.

Short working process explanation: You will be receiving payments from our customers such as wire transfers and check payments and re-transfering it to us. If you are LLC owner and you have corporate business bank account - we can give you ability to accept to payment to the tune of 500,000 USD and above.

All our activity 100% legal and follows European Union and USA Law,and was accepted by EUFA (European Union Financial Association) (Paris, 2005). Everything we offer is 100% legal.

Please if you are interested contact us immediately and forward to us your complete names, telephone phone number/fax and your full contact info.

■ ■ ■

Let's analyze this e-mail:

1 It is addressed to an unknown recipient, which means that they sent out hundreds of these and do not really know who received it.

2 They are searching for representatives who can help establish a medium of getting to their customers. *What the heck does that mean? They apparently already have customers.*

3. The job is part time, highly paid, from home. *Does this sound just too good to be true?*

4 No down payment, no investment, no special knowledge or skills. *Hey, this covers just about everybody.*

5 I need to be trusted and serious. *That's the kicker.*

6 They are going to give me ten percent of any transactions or funds received.

7 I will be receiving wire transfers and cheque payments, which I will simply re-transfer to them!

Think about this: you have a business in a country other than Canada, but you need someone in Canada to receive funds from your customers . . . just a thought, but could your customers not send you their payment *directly*, or would this make too much sense? Logically, any legitimate business or businessperson who sends goods or performs a service for a customer, no matter where in the world that customer is located, would merely invoice the customer and have payment sent directly to his or her company. Many businesses sending goods to another country would probably require full or partial payment before delivery. So why would I have my customers send payment to you, in your name? At the same time, why on earth would I give you ten percent of the monies owed, when I can have my customers pay me direct? Answer: because this is FRAUD. Neither you, nor I, nor anyone else for that matter, is going to have their customers send payment to you. This is not going to happen; this is a SCAM.

Take the case of an individual who recently lost his job. He found a job posting for a position as a "collection agent" for an overseas company. He was immediately hired, and an official-looking employment contract was couriered to him for signature. He was given a large account to collect and promised a fifteen percent commission. Amazingly, when he contacted the first debtor, he was told they would pay the $245,000 right away, and a cheque was delivered to him. He was excited to report his success to his new employer, at which time he was instructed to deposit the cheque to his own personal bank account and to wire the funds to an overseas bank account, less $36,750 (his fifteen percent) commission for one hour's work. Within days, the cheque was returned as a fraudulent item, and our friend was now on the hook for the full amount of the cheque. There was no commission; there was no legitimate job. There was no real debt owed, just a fraudulent cheque for $245,000, money he now owed to his own bank.

Look, I know you are probably tired of hearing it, but here it is once more: if you are invited to earn thousands and never leave home, or if somebody you do not know wants you to collect his money and keep some of it, this is probably fraud!

PYRAMID

. . . or is it a PONZI . . . either way, it's a SCAM.

Bernie Madoff having allegedly made off with fifty billion dollars from investors in a Ponzi scheme, I think we need to talk. I have never really seen any difference between a Ponzi and a pyramid, but one thing I do know: either way, in the end it's going to hurt!

Remember years ago, when a friend called you up and invited you to a meeting about making lots of money? Eventually you arrived at somebody's home or apartment, and they talked about a no-risk investment, huge returns, and a very small original amount of money down, to get in, etc. Now, the only thing they did *not* talk about was a product, a service, or an actual investment; just a high return at no risk. So some people bought in.

Here's how it worked: twenty or so people show up at the meeting. One person, the one doing all the talking, has already bought in for three thousand dollars, so that person is number one. The next person to buy in is number two, and so on. Let's say that fifteen people buy in, so now we have numbers one to fifteen. Number one then takes all of the money, and moves down to fifteen, and everybody else moves up one place. The new number one will host a similar meeting, with the same routine. Oh, yeah, number one has the $45,000 and, most of the time, he or she just disappears. Now if he/she stays around, number two is entitled to all of the money. Just one problem: there is no money left in the plan.

What next? It's very simple: all fifteen people recruit one person each and we have another $45,000. Number two gets that $45,000 and then moves to the bottom, and everyone else moves up one. It sure sounds great, but is anybody going to pay three thousand dollars to be number sixteen, or twenty, or twenty-five, or thirty? So now we have an unsustainable enterprise that will eventually collapse and leave a number of people with upset friends and relatives, all of whom are out three thousand dollars!

I do not want to bore you with all the differences between a Ponzi and a pyramid; suffice to say that they require a constant recruitment of people, to the point that the emphasis swings from the product or service to recruiting. In a pyramid, some of the money goes to other individuals in the scheme; in a Ponzi, the money goes to the head person.

A Ponzi gets very dangerous for you because it is draped around some sort of investment, with huge returns, limited risk, and a quick return on your money. Remember, *it does not matter what the current interest rates are, a Ponzi always offers at least seven or eight points higher.*

THE INVESTMENT INDUSTRY

How many times in your life has somebody who did not work in the investment industry given you a stock tip, or tried to get you to invest ten or twenty thousand dollars into a "can't miss" investment? We all know it happens, and the odd time it may even work out, but most of these things head south at a very rapid rate. When I worked in the RCMP Stock Market Group, we would periodically receive a complaint from somebody who had invested with his uncle, brother, brother in-law, best friend, co-worker, or somebody he had met at a bar. It does not really matter who they are—what they all have in common is what the so-called investor kept telling them, that things are really looking good . . . we should have some money soon . . . if everybody can give me just another ten thousand we can control the market

. . . the returns are really getting up there . . . just a couple more weeks, and we will have your first interest payment. This is about the time that you hear nothing further, because you cannot find the investor any longer!

This is a topic that many a book has been written about. Opportunities to defraud and take advantage abound, and the media are quick to jump on any story, or potential story, to present to readers and viewers. I will not cover this area in great detail, as again there are many great materials to review to ensure you are protected, but I will mention a few salient points in passing.

I have dealt with the same investment advisory team for almost thirty years. Are they always right? No. Are they always honest, with my best interest as the basis of all their recommendations? Yes.

How do you protect yourself against fraud and manipulation in this industry?

The IDA (Investment Dealers Association) and MFDA (Mutual Fund Dealers Association) are self-regulatory organizations that set standards of practice and a code of ethics for member institutions and advisors to follow. If you happen to be a victim of fraud by an advisor who works with an investment firm that is a member of one of these organizations, you always have the protection of the firm and not only an individual advisor. I have always dealt with an IDA member firm.

There are many examples of individual company fraud: WorldCom, Enron, Philip Services, YBM Magnex, and Bre-X to name just a few. How do you avoid significant and potentially crippling losses due to stock fraud? Diversify. The old adage that one stock can make you wealthy but lots of stocks will *keep* you wealthy is true. Many investors had financially crippling losses because they depended too much on one stock, hoping to "get rich quick" or to find the "easy money" and lost everything. Do not become one of those gamblers, but rather diversify and invest.

A friend of mine recently lost significant amounts of money on a scheme that was bought privately, not through her investment advisor. The advisor might not have caught it as a fraud, but all investments at IDA firms have to pass through a list of tests to ensure that the basic elements of a legitimate investment are present, and at the least, another pair of eyes—impartial eyes—could not hurt. You hire an advisor for a reason, for his or her advice. If the advisor cannot or will not buy an investment for you, ask why; she/he will typically be happy to explain the potential risks, or why an investment is unavailable through his/her firm. Deal with firms with a good, long-standing reputation, and well-trained, experienced, and disciplined advisors.

My best advice in this field is the simplest advice: Find somebody you like and trust, not a salesman selling performance, but a true advisor, somebody who is willing to spend the time to educate and inform you, somebody who makes the time to provide as much detail and explanation as possible. Find an advisor to whom you were referred by a friend, colleague, banker, lawyer, accountant, etc. Do not choose your advisor because he or she has the best returns (these cannot be guaranteed or perpetually repeated), but because he/she can give logical explanations and has a disciplined approach; these characteristics are repeatable.

As with any opportunity, do not invest with strangers or unknown companies over the Internet or the telephone. And remember, if it sounds too good to be true, *stay away*. I always felt that I slept better knowing that my money was out there working hard while I was sleeping, and I truly believe that proper professional investing is a great way to build wealth. Stop listening to the non-experts. Stay with the professionals and the firms that have a lengthy history in investment planning and wealth management.

12: CRIMINALS, CON ARTISTS, FRAUDSTERS, BAD GUYS, AND OTHER CREEPS

DO NOT FORGET THAT FRAUD = DECEPTION

If you have not skipped too many pages or chapters, you'll now have a pretty good idea of what is going on out there. You certainly know that to get a lot of today's fraud off the ground, the criminals need **your** help, they need good old you to get onboard; yes, they absolutely need you to pitch in and give them a hand, or their fraudulent schemes are going nowhere. Fraud without you just doesn't work—it's a dead-end street. "What am I going to do without you!" is an old lament; the answer is: not a lot.

Without you, or at least your best effort or assistance, criminals just can't get the job done. They simply can't go it alone; they have to get you to buy in at the get-go, or in the words of my sexy cousin Gichie, "It ain't happening, baby." At least it ain't happening at the start; they need a hand up from you before they can commence some type of fraudulent procedure against your assets. If you could force yourself to simply stay on the sidelines, maybe go on the DL (for you non-baseball fans, that's the disabled list) for a while, maybe quite awhile, we could eliminate a heck of a lot of today's FRAUD.

But no, you just can't seem to help yourself; you just can't stop giving out your financial information. Why so friendly, why hand them the tools they need to whack your finances? After reading most of this book, you know I don't really want to answer that question (although eventually I will have to, but maybe not right away).

Think about the words of Detective John Maciek of the Toronto Police Service. Maciek, who spent years with the Fraud Squad, mentions that after years of investigating fraud he came to the realization that CRIME DOESN'T PAY — IT COLLECTS. Just think about that comment for a minute.

Are criminals collecting from you? I sure as heck hope not, because you already know what they are going to do to get you to buy into their scams and fraudulent schemes. It does not really change at all. Yes, the central item may change, but the central theme always stays the same. The fraud is built around your winning or being selected to receive money, lots of money, or a super vacation, or lottery tickets, or a car, a house, wide-screen television, etc.

There is only one PURPOSE for this type of FRAUD, and it never, ever changes. In the words of Detective Maciek: it is to collect money from you. Put another way, it is to get you to bite, to move you to the point where you have to grab some of this, and absolutely want to send—no, *must* send—some of your money to somebody, or some information that connects them to your money, to somebody or someplace, somewhere, even if you have never heard of the place. Everybody, all together, OUCH!

Criminals simply set up some kind of scheme built around something that they are pretty sure you would love to have, even want very badly. They will tell you that you have already won it, although you never entered a contest; or they are giving you the item for a fraction of the actual cost; or they tell you that you have been selected at random. The scary part is that a lot of people just jump right in with both feet! Nobody cares that this is probably fraud; most people could not give a rat's rump about it. They just can't wait to send $99 to somebody, somewhere, so they can vacation in Florida for ten days, virtually FREE!

TALK ABOUT HEADING SOUTH! Not you—your money! These types of scams bring in tons of money, so criminals keep reworking this same old, same old. Think about it. If you keep sending the money, they will keep coming up with these types of scams forever. Yes, they may add a few new twists, a couple of new wrinkles, as we have just learned, but it really never changes. So why do you keep wading in? Why ante up? Why send them credit card info, bank account numbers, cash? Why send them anything?

Now I used to work for an old sergeant who often remarked, holy ****! These people must partake in a prolonged cocktail hour on a daily basis, or maybe they are using some of that wacky tobaccy! Either way, the good sergeant may have been on the right path! Now, when I was a third-class constable, my staff sergeant was kind enough to ask me if I believed in a fairy godmother, or the tooth fairy, or the Easter Bunny. Sorry, Good Reader, I just didn't have the guts to answer in the affirmative. Not that it wouldn't have been hilarious, but when the staff stopped laughing, the punishment would definitely have hurt! Staff also pointed out that the tooth fairy stopped leaving money when I finally left home. And come to think of it, I haven't seen the Easter Bunny since that point in time, either.

STOP believing in fairy tales! Sorry, but there is no pie in the sky, no chicken in every pot, no big ticket freebees, no contest winners for people who never entered a contest, no random selection of your name. What we do have is fees, lots and lots of fees, piled on top of more fees, piled on top of even more fees, which of course are tied into that huge **free prize** you just won. Remember, even the good old tooth fairy only left you a lousy Loonie!

All right, when we understand that FREE means FEE, we are all going to move on, right? I know that you all realize that these **feebees** (freebees with a number of fees) come by mail, e-mail, the front door, and telephone, and we are going to shred, delete, shut the door, and hang up. But never forget that they are still going to run several other scams on you, so don't let your guard down. As my old buddy Wilf liked to say, assume nothing—they may be pulling an end run!

Okay everybody, absolutely no more "it's too good to be true" fraud stuff. We are fine; nothing to worry about. We're going to be okay now. We are not going to fall for this any more, so no more risk—the criminals will just go away if we stay on the sidelines. All right, I can't trick you guys anymore, and hopefully neither can the criminals, but we all know that they have a ton of other stuff that they are going to use to try and get at your money. If one thing doesn't work, they simply upgrade to something else. They keep on working, and their frauds keep working, so we must also keep working to defend ourselves against them.

If some of the traditional fraudulent schemes stop working, then they try a little different approach.

■ ■ ■

Federal Bureau of Investigation
J Edgar Hoover Building
935 Pennsylvania Avenue, NW
Washington, D.C. 20535-0001

Payment Code: R5780906K
Reg No: 132521093
Date: March 04, 2009

NOTICE OF YOUR FUND APPROVAL

Kind Attention:

The Federal Bureau of Investigation (FBI) has discovered through our intelligence Monitoring Network that you are eligible to receive the sum of $7.5 Million USD regarding to an over-due Inheritance / Award payment which was fully endorsed to be paid in your favor.

Therefore, the Federal Bureau of Investigation in conjunction with the United States Department of Homeland Security (DHS), has screened through our various Monitoring Networks and has been confirmed and notified that the transaction you have with Spring Bank Plc is Legal and you have the Lawful Right to claim your due fund.

Please contact the Head of Operations Dr. Ferren Rodriguez, Spring Bank Plc.

Dr. Ferren Rodriguez
E-Mail

Please, be advised and be aware that your funds had been insured and the necessary charges would be taken care of by you, as confirmed by the Monitoring network.

Sincerely,

Michael German (Special Agent-in-Charge)

■ ■ ■

So now they are upgrading to the FBI and the Department of Homeland Security. But we already know that this is the same old fraud, but instead of a civilian finding money that they want to entrust to you, now it's the FBI. Remember, these criminals never give up, they just keep changing the players!

■ ■ ■

Attention,

I will like to start with reminding you that your unclaimed inheritance is still lurking around, up till now I am amazed at the way you have ignored all the notice I have sent out to you. This message will be the last notice that I will be sending out to you.

Upon the receipt of this mail I will want you to reconfirm to me your details and also tell me the reason why you have kept quiet all the while; I do believe you should have a logical answer to that. I also will like for you to know that I have some new developments on ground which I believe will be good news to you.

I will advise that you do not abandon this message and respond as a matter of urgency so that we can get done with your claim.

Best regards

Michael Graham
Associate Solicitor.

■ ■ ■

You gotta love the above! Now they are going to scold and threaten you because you do not want the funds.

■ ■ ■

ATTENTION BENEFICIARY

CONFIRMATION OF YOUR FINAL PAYMENT OF US$ 5.5M

After our crucial meeting today with the United Nation Secretary General, A committee has been put in place for the final release of all beneficiary funds in the United States and European Region. This office hereby writes to inform you that your payment has been approved for immediate release through our Foreign Accredited Finance House in Kuala Lumpur Malaysia into your account.

Our Foreign Credit Commission in KUALA LUMPUR (MALAYSIA) will release your payment within 72 hours of your accreditation.

You are advised to get back to us immediately with the below information for onward processing of your file for the Final Release Order.

Full Name
Tel & Fax #
Occupation & Age
Current Address
Your Urgent reply will highly be appreciated

Yours faithfully.
Prof. Marcus Bruno

■ ■ ■

Just in case you forgot, the above e-mail is the same old stuff—a little refresher for you.

■ ■ ■

China National Chemicals Import & Export Corporation (SINOCHEM)
Tower A2, Fuxingmenai,
Street, Beijing,
People's Republic of China.
PC: 100080.

REF: SC/09/00867546.

Dear Sir/Madam,

We need Representatives from all over the World and as specified.

North America

Collection Officer wanted in this region who will assist in retrieving debts from our clients in USA & CANADA.

EUROPE, ASIA, SOUTH AMERICA & AUSTRALIAS

Someone needed to assist in setting up a Branch of our Company in his/her country.

If interested, please supply the following:

1) Name
2) Country

Send your response via email SPECIFICALLY to Respectfully Submitted,
Mr. Liu Deshu.
President.
Sinochem Trading Company

■ ■ ■

Dear Sir/Madam,

I am Mr Wang Peijun, managing director of Yancheng Jiangyang Foreign Trade Engine Co. Ltd. We are a trading company that is into the import and export of goods like Generating Sets, Engine, and Air Compresso Set etc, we export these equipments in tons into U.S, Canada and Europe. Owing to the large amount of clients that we have in the U.S.A/ Canada we are having difficulty in reaching all of them, therefore we decided to employ representatives in all the states of America, Canada, Europe to help us get to our clients. As our representative, you shall serve as a link between us and our clients and you will also be responsible for the collection of payments on our behalf. Note: that you shall have a 10% commission for every payment that you collect on our behalf. Kindly fill this form below and forward to this E-mail address:

1.FIRST NAMES :

2.MIDDLE NAME :

3.CONTACT ADDRESS :

4.PHONE NUMBER :

5.FAX NUMBER:

6.COUNTRY OF RESIDENCE:

7.OCCUPATION:

8.MARITAL STATUS:

9.EMAIL ADDRESS:

Subject to your response, we shall have our company's attorney draft out
an agreement to seal up this contract.

Best Regards,
Mr Wang Peijun

■ ■ ■

At a time when many people are looking for a job, and have their resumes out there in cyberspace, the above type of job offer presents extreme danger. NEVER open a bank account in your own name for anyone else, and never deposit cheques into your own personal account for any company or organization. Company A is never going to pay outstanding invoices owed to Company B by sending Company B a cheque to *you*, with you as the payee. This is FRAUD.

HOME RENOVATION AND REPAIR

I want to specifically mention home renovation and repair fraud. This has always been a problem, and now with the federal government's Home Renovation Tax Credit, I suspect even more criminals will get involved in this type of fraud.

When I first joined the RCMP, I lived in barracks. Believe me, renovations were needed, and I suspect renovations or repairs would be a good idea at most of the places where you all live. Just remember that this is an old con game and be very careful whom you deal with. In fact, let me give you some rules:

1   Get three estimates; do not let other contractors see those estimates or tell them the amounts.

2   Ask how long the contractor has been in business.

3   Get the business address and telephone number, make sure the address is not a mail drop, and make sure the telephone is not a cell phone.

4   Find out if the contractor has his own trucks and equipment.

5   Get some references and check them out.

6   Check to see if the contractor is listed in the telephone book.

7   Be very leery if you are being rushed or pushed to sign up immediately.

8   Get a contract drawn up.

9   If the contractor is working in your area, talk to the
     homeowners after the contractor has left for the day.

COUNTRY GIRLS
(THE FOREIGN COUNTRY GIRLS SCAM)

Hey Guys: you, me, and God know you just can't beat a good old
country gal. Come on, those beauties from Picture Butte or Beaver-
lodge, Alberta, or those chicks from Chicoutimi PQ, those ladies
from Lucknow or Mattawa, Ontario; or how about the babes of
Bridesville or Fanny Bay, BC. Hey, let's not forget Tatamagouche
or Dingwall, Nova Scotia, Pouch Cove and Buchans, Newfound-
land, and yes, those lovelies from Biggar or Choiceland, Saskatch-
ewan!

Yes, the country is overflowing with divas and hotties, but
Gentlemen, before we go much further, let's have a little talk,
just between us boys. This is Canada, home to the world's most
gorgeous women—what's not to love? But no, for whatever
reason, some of you guys want to look outside our borders . . .
sort of move into foreign territory . . . start a relationship with
some of those **exciting girls from other countries.**

Now, dating and mating in foreign places sure sounds
exotic, but it is also one of the greatest fraudulent minefields
that one could ever venture into. Even I realize love is blind, but
try very hard not to fall head over heels in love on the Internet,
while reading the mail, or while talking long distance on the
telephone.

Sometimes the truth hurts, but if you have gotten on in
years, you have probably been there a few times already. Now,
please remember that I'm not talking about you the great book-
buyer, but more likely a friend, an acquaintance, or co-worker.
But here's the thing: if somebody is thirty-five, forty, or beyond,
and he has not had any success whatsoever with dating the most
foxy, gorgeous, beautiful women he has ever seen (he hasn't
gotten to first base), it probably is not going to happen now. If
every time he approaches a hottie she totally ignores him, or if
she asks him to call her a cab so she can leave, or she mentions

that she is not into guys, it's a bad, bad sign. And if he has not been doing great with the ladies at home, he is probably going to be in the same boat if he looks overseas.

Keeping in mind that Internet scams and ID fraud are very prevalent, you might want to think about where some of these foreign bride and girlfriend sites are actually located. Are the women whose photos appear on the site legitimate, or are their photos being utilized without their knowledge? Maybe that beauty from Russia or the Philippines is really some guy in Scarborough running another scam. Unless I have missed something in life, those young, middle-aged, or older beauties already have more guys than they need, and at the very end of the day, they are probably not looking to add any more men to their daily routine.

Many women from poor parts of the world may not have a computer or the Internet; they may not speak, read, or write English, and they may not have unfettered access to a telephone in the home. Hopefully we all understand that if I run a site with photos of ten gorgeous gals who indicate they are looking for husbands in America, I will get thousands of hits. You are not the only guy in the world corresponding with these lovelies. You are not the only person trying to befriend, date, or marry them; I say marry, although my guess is that at least some of these gorgeous gals are already married! Very hard to be hot and single.

Let's not shoot the messenger, but somebody needs to throw a little rain on this parade—in fact, maybe a few buckets of water to cool things to the point where you can consider the following when caught up in an FDF (a foreign dating frenzy) . . . and yes, the same thing will apply to *anyone* you have met on the Internet but never face to face.

You will remember that I have hammered home the fact that somebody you have never met, somebody that you do not know, wants to give you ten million dollars to keep for them, and this is a scam. This situation is somewhat the same: somebody you do not really know, someone you have never met, after a couple of e-mails, or letters, over a couple of weeks, mentions that she is falling in LOVE with little old you. Keep in mind that the e-mails or letters could have been written by employees of the agency the gal is with, and not by her. Be careful if the agency is charging you a fee for letters or e-mails from her and to her. Try and get her telephone number. If either the agency or your gal refuse to give you her telephone number, maybe it's time to rethink what you are doing.

I almost hate to bring this up, but if a site offers free correspondence with its gorgeous brides-to-be, I can almost guarantee you this is just another feebee. Yes, before you can start dreaming about your new relationship, they are going to add in a ton of fees. The final nail in the coffin is always when your new gal asks to borrow money, or needs money for an operation for a family member, or . . . hey, never mind the reason—a request for money comes in. You should be heading out the front door and spending more of your time with our **Canadian Cuties**!

13: THE CRIMINAL QUIZ, OR WHAT'RE YOU GOING TO DO NOW?

I could write this as a reverse kiss of death, but let's start off in the normal way. Here is the first scenario: morning arrives, usually too quickly, you get up, grab yourself a bottle of water, put the news on, and all of a sudden the telephone rings. It's the friendly bank inspector and he needs your help to catch a crooked employee. Just so you know, this friendly but crooked bank inspector is going to require you to withdraw several hundred dollars from your account. Don't ask me, I have no idea how your withdrawing several hundred dollars of your own money will help catch anybody, but if you do this, you will definitely feel the reverse kiss of death.

Do you:

A   Mention that you're just too tired to help, and suggest he call the police, or his own bank investigators?

B   Ask if you could assist him right after you finish your day shift with the local police force?

C   Tell him to call your lawyer?

D   Indicate that you would love to help, but you do not have any money to withdraw?

E   Just hang up and save your breath?

So tell me, what are you going to do? Exactly—let that call go to the answering machine. No financial institution is going to solicit your help to catch a bad employee. Yes, this is the good old phony bank inspector call; I just wanted to give you some options in case you could not bring yourself to just **hang up.**

All right, can we have the next telephone call, please? Okay, you've just arrived home, you walk into the kitchen, and the phone rings; this time it's the police, or at least it is somebody *saying* he is the police. They need your chequing account information and PIN.

Do you:

A   Ask if this is for the Annual Summer Police Dance and Pig Roast?

B   Ascertain if maybe they also need another form of revenue?

C   Mention that the chief is your brother-in-law?

D   Tell them you can't remember your PIN?

E   Just **hang up** and get yourself something to eat?

Hanging up is always good. The police are not going to ask you for personal financial information, but a good rule of thumb is this: if somebody calls and tells you he is the police, ask for his rank and badge number, the squad he works in and his extension. Now hang up, call the main police non-emergency number, and ask for the extension number you were just given.

I almost hate to say this, but there is another telephone call coming (you probably already knew that). This time it is somebody who tells you she is calling from your credit card company, and she needs to verify your mother's maiden name.

Do you:

A   Ask her what happened to the records that already contain this information?

B   Request a supervisor so you can find out what the heck is going on?

C   Get this person's name, department, and telephone number and then hang up?

D   Stay away from the kiss of death and never answer this question?

E   **Just hang up?**

If anyone calls you about *anything* to do with a credit card, utilize the tried and true method: just hang up! Now, if you start to worry that there may be a problem with your card, simply call the telephone number on the back of your card, tell them what happened, and ask if everything is okay.

I don't want to bore you with the rest of this stuff, so let me lump it all together. If anybody calls you and indicates he or she is a government official, a lawyer, an investigator, etc., and tries to solicit personal or financial information, get his/her name, department, and telephone number, and then hang up. If you want to pursue this any further, get the telephone number from the telephone book. **Never, ever call the number that he/she supplied.**

You're up and about, you turn on the computer, and there is an e-mail message from a financial institution. Something about unauthorized attempts on your account, and they want you to follow the link and enter your name and password or they are going to block your account access.

Do you:

A   Panic and then freak out?

B   Realize you have no money in your account anyway?

C   Give yourself the Kiss of Death and follow that link and then input your password?

D   Pat yourself on the back because you caught another attempt at fraud?

E   Just **delete**?

Nothing feels better than the good old DELETE. The financial institution already has your password—they are never going to ask you for it! This is fraud. **Just delete. Do not get spoofed.**

The telephone is ringing, you are trying to get through your e-mails, and now somebody knocks at your front door. Talk about your lucky day, and yes, it is a home renovator who is working in your area. Now this could be a good thing, depending on what he has to say. He asks if you live alone, then asks if he can look inside the home, stating that you can get big savings because their equipment is in the neighbourhood, and you will also get a senior's discount. But—and this is a huge but—to get this special price, you have to sign today and pay fifty percent of the total cost of the job up front.

Do you:

A   Ask if this is his first day on the job?

B   Ask if he took the old math?

C   Mention you are positive you are now going to sign up for the do-it-yourself home renovations classes at Home Depot?

D   Request that he come back tomorrow when your son who is with the City Police Fraud Squad will be home?

E   Just close the door when he starts to pressure you?

Always get three estimates from established companies, never pay more than ten percent up front, never let anyone you do not know into your home, do not deal with anyone **pressuring you to sign now**. Always talk it over with a relative, a friend, or a lawyer before you sign anything.

Finally, the day is almost over, you get home, grab the mail, and . . . holy cow, you just won five thousand dollars in a contest that you never entered! Talk about horseshoes! This is simply outstanding, I think. Okay, but there is also a small catch: you have to send a cheque for $343 to cover the administration cost before they will send you the five thousand.

Do you:

A   Break open the piggy bank and hope you have $343 in pennies?

B   Wonder if you should you call Mom and borrow the money, so at least when you lose it, you're not out anything?

C   Maybe re-gift the letter?

D   Work on the premise that you really are a winner and this is totally legitimate?

E   Make an appointment with your shrink if you are going the "D" route?

Now, you could write back and tell them to take the $343 out of the cheque before they send it to you. Or better still, tear that letter up. This is **fraud**.

Staff Sergeant Jim V. Bennett, RCMP "E" Division Veteran Member, put it best when he said that in Canada you have the ability to either stay on the fraud sidelines, or, if you would like to take a shot at a very large something for almost nothing, you can also pick your own poison (another nice kiss of death). That way, the only unknown in the whole equation becomes how long it is going to take you to try and get your money back, provided you can actually live long enough to recover anything!

Now, just in case you've received another letter from a credit card company offering you a credit card, or something from the federal government with your SIN number written in the header, remember that before you throw these in the recycling, you need to shred them and anything else that contains personal or financial information.

Let me finish off here by talking about what can happen when we combine a few fraudsters with identity theft—the classic enemy within. There are a number of investigations involving individuals looking for employment, and at a time when many people have lost jobs, this type of scam will just keep evolving as the economy worsens. It does not matter if you are unemployed, a summer student, or simply attempting to get a higher-paying job—you must be careful out there.

Remember, there are tons of fraudulent scams revolving around your getting some type of job. A lot of these scams start off with things like guaranteed employment, work from home, work in foreign countries, a job guaranteed after training, and the "Hey, we want you to work in America for our foreign company!" A lot of these are front-end loaded with fees; usually there are no guarantees, just lots of fees. Be careful. And remember, the only thing really guaranteed in life is the fact that in most cases you are the author of your own demise!

I worked on an investigation involving the hiring of truck drivers. Somebody advertised in some newspapers that they were hiring long-haul drivers and indicated that anyone interested should be at a specific address between nine a.m. and five p.m. on the 14th of April. Everyone who applied had to fill out an application, have a brief interview, and leave his driver's licence with the application. They were all instructed to return the next day to pick up their licences. You probably already know the rest of the story, but I will tell you anyway: Yes, when everyone returned the next day, the office was closed and vacant; another classic identity theft scam!

Just a word of caution: Until you have been hired, be very careful about what information and identification you give to a potential employer, particularly if you are not in the human resources office of an established company.

Perhaps in the past few years you have been at a conference, convention, or sporting event. If so, you have no doubt seen the people trying to give you a t-shirt, or a hat, or a towel etc., if you will just sign up for a credit card. Yes, they fill out a credit card application with you, and you get that great free gift. You may also become a victim of identity theft if the completed applications are not protected during the event. Many times I have seen a box of completed applications sitting on the floor without anyone standing close to it; we probably all know somebody who completed an application in a public place and then became another identity fraud victim.

If nothing else, you, the great book buyers, realize that FRAUD and IDENTITY THEFT come in all different shapes and sizes, and they are very adaptable. There is no script for fraud; it can be in the form of a telephone call, an e-mail, a letter, or a knock at your door. It can be as a result of someone's taking your garbage, mail, wallet or handbag, or the skimming of your credit or debit card. It could even be a friend, relative, or co-worker who either takes over your identity, or gets you unknowingly into some fraudulent scheme. There are no boundaries; nothing is off-limits, from your blue box to your cell phone, your garage door opener to your debit card, your computer to your chequing account. Fraud is everywhere and it is very difficult to stop, at least initially.

But remember, it is quite easy to detect and easier still to prevent. Yes, **you** are the first line of defence; you have to do some of the grunt work, but who better than **you** to do some of the checking on you and your family?

When I joined the RCMP, I started in the stables. Believe me, nobody at "N" Division had it better than the horses, thanks in large part to the constables. You good readers get to start at a much higher level, and with you helping yourself, your personal finances should stay at a much higher level than the good old stable floor (by the way, that was a spotless stable floor!). Part of playing keep-away with fraud is understanding what things to avoid (knowing when to say no) and completing a bit of daily maintenance on your financial products.

I want to share with you some things that will throw a monkey wrench into the bad guys' fraudulent tricks. Foiling fraudsters just seems to make for a much better day. So hold on, everyone: our criminal prevention program is about to commence.

OKAY, SO YOU WANT TO KEEP THE FRAUDSTERS AT BAY —
MAYBE WHACK THEM BEFORE THEY MAKE YOU PAY?
THEN HERE ARE ELEVEN WAYS TO COMPEL THESE CREEPS
TO CALL IT A DAY, SO YOU'LL NEVER HAVE TO PAY OR SAY,
"HONEY, DO YOU HAVE THE NUMBER FOR THE FRAUD SQUAD?"

1   If a stranger contacts you who selected you at random and wants to give you anything of value . . . **say no.**

2   If a stranger contacts you who selected you at random and wants to invest your money . . . **say no.**

3.   If a stranger contacts you and tells you that you're a big contest winner, even though you did not enter the contest and have no idea what he or she is talking about . . . **say goodbye.**

4   If a stranger contacts you and requests money for some charitable organization that you have never heard of . . . **it's a no.**

5   If you receive an e-mail from a prince, or a lawyer, or a minister, etc, and he wants to send you a few million to keep for him . . . **it's a DELETE.**

6   If you receive an e-mail from a financial institution requiring you to log on to their secure site and input your password, etc. . . . another **DELETE.**

7   If a stranger contacts you and has a deal that is just too good to be true, remember, it *isn't* . . . **just walk away.**

8   Protect your mail with a lock, shred anything you are sending to the garbage, and lock up all of your identification that is not on your person!

9   When you use an ATM, or point-of-sale, terminal, use your body or your other hand to shield your PIN.

10   You be the detective. Solve your own crime and hammer the criminals before you get hammered. Every day, via **Internet banking,** check the debits to your credit cards, check all activity in your credit union and bank accounts, and immediately contact your financial institution if you even suspect there is a problem.

11   Check your credit history frequently. Look at the inquiries section and report any problems immediately. Remember, some of the credit unions and banks already have programs in place to help you in this regard.

OH, AND HEY, GUYS, STOP HELPING THEM!

14: THIS IS JUST THE BEGINNING—I WILL SEE YOU ALL AGAIN, I PROMISE!

Well, we have come to the end of the book. Hopefully you are all saying, "Aw, shucks, that was a great read. I was hoping it would never end!" Okay, maybe I'm a little biased, but if you gained some knowledge and at the same time were entertained, it's all to the good! In police work, we like to say a little knowledge is dangerous, but in your case a lot of knowledge is going to be very dangerous to the criminals.

Great job, everybody! Give yourselves a pat on the back! You can put the book down now, but let me ask you something—okay, but before I do that, take a little break, grab a bottle of water, your significant other, maybe take a little walk . . . why not do something you may not have done for a while, like visit the neighbours, and hopefully they won't have a heart attack when they see you at the door.

All right, you're back, you're hydrated, had some exercise, some "we" time, and if your neighbour did not shut the door in your face, it's all good. However, I have to tell you that this is kind of a sad moment for me; yes, I'm feeling a little upset, because collectively, this is our last fireside chat. Now, having said that, you may want the old staff sergeant to come to your office, church, service organization, or residence (if you can get 100 book buyers to come over as well) to sign his book for everybody, so hopefully we will meet again.

Now sit back, put your feet up, and relax. Are you, Good Reader, thinking the same thing I am? Yes, yes, of course, I knew it. Having read the book, we are all on the same page, we are all at the same level, and yes, you are all thinking the same thing I am, I knew it! Yes, collectively we can eradicate fraud and fraudsters! Just imagine how great your world would be if you could keep all of your money for yourself; no more sleepless nights, no more suckers' lists, no more payday loans, all your dough stays with you. I really believe that together we can do it—yes, we can eliminate fraud; I know we can.

Just before I go 10-7, I want to tell you about some very important channels that I have set up for your benefit. If you would like to share some information or a story on some scams or fraudulent schemes, please send me your stories and I will include some of them in my next book, although I will not include your name without your permission. I would like to know where the fraud or attempted fraud took place. Simply e-mail me at **terry. keighley@sympatico.ca**. Or you can write to me at Staff Terry, P.O. Box 624, Streetsville, Ontario, Canada, L5M 2C1.

If for any reason you require professional advice or assistance, or have problems that you cannot resolve, remember you are not alone; help is on the way, and help is as close as my Web site. Contact me at any time at **www.staffterry.com**.

Oh, one more thing: Thank you so much for your support! It is truly appreciated.

Best Regards

Staff Sergeant Terry Keighley
Royal Canadian Mounted Police
"O" Division Veteran Member

TERRY'S PHOTO GALLERY

Keighley thinking about his next touchdown—
with the RCMP football team in Ottawa.

Keighley speaking with Princess Ann.

Keighley (Left) at the Miss Universe 1982 dress rehearsal, with Karen Baldwin.

Keighley receiving Long Service Medal from the commanding officer of "O" Division, 1984.

S/Sgt Keighley on the deck of the Royal Yacht Britannia.

Keighley on guard at the Economic Summit; U.S. President Reagan in foreground.

Keighley working hard in St. Vincent and the Grenadines.

Saturday morning in the dugout, 14 August 1999; Blue Jays manager,
Jim Fregosi, with "Hulk Hogan," aka Staff Keighley.

Detective Maciek, Cindy Lauper, and Keighley.

About the Author

Terry Keighley was born in Brantford, Ontario, where he attended Pauline Johnson Collegiate. Keighley served Canada as a member of the Royal Canadian Mounted Police for over twenty-five years. His last ten years were spent at the Toronto Commercial Crime Section, where he retired as a Staff Sergeant. During his RCMP service, Staff Keighley received the Long Service Metal.

Staff Sergeant Terry Keighley is a graduate of the University of Toronto and has spent most of his working life dealing with victims of fraudulent practices. Keighley lives in the Greater Toronto Area and works as both a security consultant and a private investigator. He has two daughters, Taija and Katriina, and a son, Christian.